INTERNATIONAL JUDICIAL REVIEW

The book is motivated by a question: When should international courts intervene in domestic affairs? To answer this question thoroughly, it is broken down to a series of separate inquiries: When is intervention legitimate? When can international courts identify good legal solutions? When will intervention initiate useful processes? When will it lead to good outcomes? These inquiries are answered based on reviewing judgments of international courts, strategic analysis, and empirical findings. The book outlines under which conditions intervention by international courts is recommended and evaluates the implications international courts have for society.

SHAI DOTHAN is Associate Professor of International and Public Law at the University of Copenhagen, Faculty of Law affiliated with iCourts – the Centre of Excellence for International Courts. He is the author of *Reputation and Judicial Tactics: A Theory of National and International Courts* (Cambridge University Press, 2015).

STUDIES ON INTERNATIONAL COURTS AND TRIBUNALS

General Editors
Andreas Føllesdal, University of Oslo
Geir Ulfstein, University of Oslo

Studies on International Courts and Tribunals contains theoretical and interdisciplinary scholarship on legal aspects as well as the legitimacy and effectiveness of international courts and tribunals.

Other books in the series:

Mads Andenas and Eirik Bjorge (eds.) *A Farewell to Fragmentation: Reassertion and Convergence in International Law*

Cecilia M. Bailliet and Nobuo Hayashi (eds.) *The Legitimacy of International Criminal Tribunals*

Amrei Müller with Hege Elisabeth Kjos (eds.) *Judicial Dialogue and Human Rights*

Nienke Grossman, Harlan Grant Cohen, Andreas Follesdal and Geir Ulfstein (eds.) *Legitimacy and International Courts*

Robert Howse, Hélène Ruiz-Fabri , Geir Ulfstein and Michelle Q. Zang (eds.) *The Legitimacy of International Trade Courts and Tribunals*

Theresa Squatrito, Oran Young, Andreas Føllesdal and Geir Ulfstein (eds.) *The Performance of International Courts and Tribunals*

Marlene Wind (ed.) *International Courts and Domestic Politics*

Christina Voigt (ed.) *International Judicial Practice on the Environment: Questions of Legitimacy*

Freya Baetens (ed.) *Legitimacy of Unseen Actors in International Adjudication*

Martin Scheinin (ed.) *Human Rights Norms in 'Other' International Courts*

INTERNATIONAL JUDICIAL REVIEW

When Should International Courts Intervene?

SHAI DOTHAN
University of Copenhagen

CAMBRIDGE
UNIVERSITY PRESS

CAMBRIDGE
UNIVERSITY PRESS

University Printing House, Cambridge CB2 8BS, United Kingdom

One Liberty Plaza, 20th Floor, New York, NY 10006, USA

477 Williamstown Road, Port Melbourne, VIC 3207, Australia

314–321, 3rd Floor, Plot 3, Splendor Forum, Jasola District Centre, New Delhi – 110025, India

79 Anson Road, #06–04/06, Singapore 079906

Cambridge University Press is part of the University of Cambridge.

It furthers the University's mission by disseminating knowledge in the pursuit of education, learning, and research at the highest international levels of excellence.

www.cambridge.org
Information on this title: www.cambridge.org/9781108488761
DOI: 10.1017/9781108771795

First published 2020

Printed in the United Kingdom by TJ International Ltd, Padstow Cornwall

A catalogue record for this publication is available from the British Library.

Library of Congress Cataloging-in-Publication Data
Names: Dothan, Shai, author.
Title: International judicial review : when should international courts intervene? / Shai Dothan.
Description: 1. | New York : Cambridge University Press, 2020. | Series: Studies on international courts and tribunals | Includes bibliographical references and index.
Identifiers: LCCN 2019038296 (print) | LCCN 2019038297 (ebook) | ISBN 9781108488761 (hardback) | ISBN 9781108738828 (paperback) | ISBN 9781108771795 (epub)
Subjects: LCSH: International courts. | Jurisdiction (International law)
Classification: LCC KZ6250 .D68 2020 (print) | LCC KZ6250 (ebook) | DDC 341.5/5–dc23
LC record available at https://lccn.loc.gov/2019038296
LC ebook record available at https://lccn.loc.gov/2019038297

ISBN 978-1-108-48876-1 Hardback

To Melinda

CONTENTS

ACKNOWLEDGMENTS

You may not be interested in international courts, but international courts – to paraphrase Trotsky's famous aphorism – are interested in you. They can determine the borders of your country. They influence the price you pay for your groceries. They can protect your basic human rights. They may even, more often than not indirectly, get you in prison. International courts have a lot of power and this power has to be justified, regulated, and – sometimes – limited. That is what this book is about.

I am interested in international courts. In fact, I spent the last five years as an associate professor of international and public law at iCourts – the Danish National Research Foundation's Centre of Excellence for International Courts at the University of Copenhagen, Faculty of Law. The book has been written over these five years as have some of the publications leading to it. I thank Mikael Rask Madsen, the director of iCourts, for his constant help and support during that period. iCourts is funded by the Danish National Research Foundation Grant no. DNRF105.

Before coming to iCourts, I did research at the Max Planck Institute for Comparative Public Law and International Law; Tel Aviv University Faculty of Law at the Global Trust Research Project directed by Professor Eyal Benvenisti and funded by an ERC Advanced Grant; the Hebrew University of Jerusalem Faculty of Law at the Research Group on Effective International Adjudication directed by Professor Yuval Shany and funded by a European Research Council Starting Grant for Frontier Research; and the University of Chicago Law School. In all these places, I have written about a series of topics related to the question: When should international courts intervene in domestic affairs? This question is the focus of the book.

Chapter 2 of the book draws on my papers *In Defence of Expansive Interpretation in the European Court of Human Rights*, 3 Cambridge J. Int'l & Comp. L. 508 (2014); *The Three Traditional Approaches to Treaty Interpretation: A Current Application to the European Court of Human Rights*, 42 Fordham Int'l L. J. 765 (2019).

Chapter 3 draws on my papers: *The Optimal Use of Comparative Law*, 43 DENV. J. INT'L L. & POL'Y. 21 (2014); *Three Interpretive Constraints on the European Court of Human Rights*, *in* THE RULE OF LAW AT THE NATIONAL AND INTERNATIONAL LEVELS: CONTESTATIONS AND DEFERENCE 227 (Machiko Kanetake & André Nollkaemper eds., 2016); *The Advantage of International Courts*, 31 BAR ILAN UNIVERSITY LAW REVIEW 675 (2018) (Hebrew); *Comparative Views on the Right to Vote in International Law: The Case of Prisoners' Disenfranchisement*, *in* COMPARATIVE INTERNATIONAL LAW 379 (Anthea Roberts et al. eds., 2018); *Judicial Deference Allows European Consensus to Emerge*, 18 CHI. J. INT'L. L. 392 (2018).

Chapter 4 draws on my paper *International Courts Improve Public Deliberation*, 39 MICH. J. INT'L L. 217 (2018).

Chapter 5 draws on my papers: *Luring NGOs to International Courts: A Comment on CLR v. Romania*, 75 HEIDELBERG J. INT'L L. 635 (2015); *A Virtual Wall of Shame: The New Way of Imposing Reputational Sanctions on Defiant States*, 27 DUKE J. COMP. & INT'L. L. 141 (2017); *Social Networks and the Enforcement of International Law*, *in* EDWARD ELGAR RESEARCH HANDBOOK ON THE SOCIOLOGY OF INTERNATIONAL LAW 333 (Moshe Hirsch & Andrew Lang eds., 2018).

Chapter 6 draws on my paper *Deterring War Crimes*, 40 N. C. J. INT'L L. & COM. REG. 739 (2015).

I have taught a seminar on international courts at the Hebrew University of Jerusalem Faculty of Law and a course titled "International Organizations" at the University of Copenhagen, Faculty of Law. The discussions with my students in these courses were very useful for sharpening my thinking about some of the topics addressed in this book.

I thank Karen J. Alter, Patrick Barry, Or Bassok, Eyal Benvenisti, Lisa Bernstein, David Thor Bjørgvinsson, Armin von Bogdandy, Mikkel Jarle Christensen, Avinoam Cohen, Yoav Dothan, Federico Fabbrini, Olga Frishman, Rotem Giladi, Tom Ginsburg, Francoise Hampson, Laurence R. Helfer, Jakob v. H. Holtermann, Mikael Rask Madsen, Christopher McCrudden, Ioannis Panagis, Anne Peters, Ariel Porat, W. Michael Reisman, and Yuval Shany for many instructive conversations and comments.

My biggest debt of gratitude is to my wife, Melinda Dothan. I thank her not only for helping me every day to concentrate on my work, but mainly for inspiring with her beauty everything that I write, including this book. I dedicate the book to her.

1

Introduction

A The Problem with International Courts

The beginning of the twenty-first century has seen an unprecedented growth in the power and influence of international courts. These courts have increased in number, they have expanded their scope, and the amount of cases they decide is rapidly multiplying. Many commentators criticize this development.

These commentators present a series of arguments against the increased intervention of international courts in domestic affairs:

- Some argue that international courts lack democratic legitimacy: These courts are unelected, unrepresentative bodies and should therefore keep out of the business of democracies that usually represent the interests of their citizens.
- Another common criticism is that international courts are unlikely to make better decisions than national governments. In fact, some argue that these courts have poorer institutional capacities than national bodies and should therefore not intervene in their affairs.
- One can also argue that taking important issues out of the hands of representative bodies weakens public deliberation, which is essential for a healthy democracy.
- Other commentators call attention to the danger that international courts are captured by powerful transnational interest groups – some of which may be organized as Non-Governmental Organizations (NGOs) – and serve the interests of these elites instead of those of the general public.
- Finally, there are those who argue that the ultimate outcome of international courts' intervention, after all relevant actors in the global arena have reacted to their judgments and decisions, may be far worse than if the international court didn't intervene at all.

These arguments are often used by politicians to attack international courts and to threaten them with ignoring their judgments or even leaving their jurisdiction. The incredibly prolific European Court of Human Rights (ECHR), which disposed of more than 85,000 cases in 2017 alone, is often in the line of fire. So is the far less productive International Criminal Court (ICC), which managed to convict only eight people in more than sixteen years. Other courts that drew significant criticism are the Court of Justice of the European Union (CJEU) and the World Trade Organization Appellate body (WTO AB).

This book is a rejoinder to the critics of intervention by international courts. It highlights the conditions under which the judgments of international courts are both legitimate and likely to trigger the formation of good policies. It argues that international courts can enhance, instead of stifle, public deliberation. It suggests how international courts can cooperate with other actors in the global arena in ways that minimize the risk of capture and are likely to lead to good outcomes. The arguments against international courts are not dismissed. Rather, the book studies the boundaries and limitations of these arguments and explains when international courts should and should not intervene.

B Overview of the Book

Chapter 2 addresses the legitimacy of judicial law-making by international courts. International courts are constructed by states or international organizations to interpret and apply certain legal provisions. As far as courts only apply existing law, one may argue that they do nothing but execute the mandate that was duly given to them. Yet when international courts apply the law, they often develop it in ways that were unsanctioned, and often unforeseen, by their creators. Add to that the fact that even international courts that are not legally bound by their previous judgments often rely on their own judgments as if they were binding precedents and it is impossible to escape the conclusion that international courts make law all the time.

As judicial bodies, international courts are bound by the treaties that created them. These treaties are the formal basis for the courts' authority. Courts cannot contradict them in their judgments. However, international courts can use methods of expansive interpretation to manipulate the meaning of their founding documents. Expansive interpretation does not constitute a breach of the limits of the courts' authority, but it still raises the problem of democratic legitimacy of these courts. The problem emerges because international courts are not constructed to represent the public in the states under their jurisdiction. They must therefore justify any use of their interpretative powers to intervene in the decisions of elected bodies in democratic states.

International courts ought to interpret their founding treaties restrictively only as long as these treaties adequately represent the interests of all the people affected by them. This may not be the case if the provisions for amending the treaty make it very difficult to change it in light of either new conditions or shifting preferences of the majority of the treaty's member states. Such provisions often give unmerited extortive power to a minority of states that resist any amendment to the treaty. Additionally, even if states can easily change the treaty, states may not always properly represent individuals. All democracies may be subject to democratic failures such as lack of political power for national minorities, disenfranchisement of vulnerable groups such as foreigners and in some countries prisoners, and immense power concentrated by interest groups. When treaties do not represent the will of states or when states do not represent the will of individuals, expansive interpretation doesn't necessarily contradict the will of all affected people and is therefore legitimate.

Chapter 3 addresses the second major challenge to intervention by international courts: the argument that there is no reason to believe their decisions would be better than those of national bodies. The book makes no claim about the legal proficiency of international judges. Instead, it addresses the problem indirectly by arguing that the unique institutional position of international courts helps guide the international community in the right direction. Therefore, even if the decision-making abilities of international judges aren't any better than those of national judges or politicians, allowing international courts to intervene would lead to better laws and policies than blocking their intervention.

The argument in Chapter 3 relies on the intuition that if many states adopt a certain policy, this policy is probably a good one. Eric Posner and Cass Sunstein used this intuition to construct a justification for the use of comparative law by national courts.[1] They apply the Condorcet Jury Theorem – a simple mathematical model according to which a majority's decision in a group is more likely to be correct than the decision of any individual decision-maker, at least under certain conditions. Unfortunately for Posner and Sunstein's argument, one of the conditions for the

[1] Eric Posner & Cass Sunstein, *The Law of Other States*, 59 STAN. L. REV. 131 (2006).

applicability of the Jury Theorem is that decision-makers in the group decide independently. This conflicts with their own recommendation to states because they call on states to learn from the laws adopted by each other, violating the condition of independence. Due to this problem, the use of comparative law by national courts may prove self-defeating. It would result in states following each other's decisions without making any independent judgment, what Posner and Sunstein call "information cascades."

These cascades can be solved by international courts – not because they are better decision-makers but simply because their institutional position can preempt the problem. For example, the ECHR applies a doctrine called "emerging consensus." According to this doctrine, the court finds states that violate human rights that are protected by the majority of states in Europe in violation of the European Convention on Human Rights – the text it is tasked with applying. The ECHR follows the majority of the states and therefore, in line with the Jury Theorem logic, aggregates their collective wisdom. At the same time, states can decide independently, knowing that they can be guided by the ECHR. Some empirical research suggests states actually act this way, and wait for the ECHR's decision before they change their laws to conform to the European majority's view.[2]

The intervention of the ECHR breaks the vicious circle that states were locked into. It allows states, on the one hand, to decide independently and fulfill the critical condition for the applicability of the Jury Theorem and, on the other hand, to enjoy the benefits of comparative law by following the ECHR's judgments. However, this solution will work well only to the extent that the states do not have conflicting interests that would motivate them not to decide independently. If states want to adopt good policies quickly, before the ECHR has a chance to intervene, they may attempt to use comparative law themselves and start an information cascade. To the extent that the ECHR may delay or manipulate its decisions to avoid a political backlash, this problem may prove severe.

As a possible solution, the ECHR may use its margin of appreciation doctrine, which allows it to issue guidelines for the states' behavior while still deferring to state policies and not finding a violation. The court can thus escape the risk of a hostile response and be able to rapidly and

[2] *See* Laurence R. Helfer & Erik Voeten, *International Courts as Agents of Legal Change: Evidence from LGBT Rights in Europe*, 68 INT'L ORG. 77, 106 (2014).

honestly apply emerging consensus, motivating states to act independently and wait for the court's final decision. The margin of appreciation doctrine also allows the ECHR to provide states with a warning that their practices contradict the European majority without accusing them of violating the convention. This may increase the willingness of states to decide independently instead of trying to guess the court's future judgments and conform to them in advance. The ECHR may also be justified in using the margin of appreciation doctrine if there is good reason to believe that the examined state could make better policy by itself, or if this state is too different from the rest of Europe to make learning from other European states useful. This set of considerations can determine the boundaries for the intervention of the ECHR in state policies and the court's optimal level of deference to certain policies of the states.

There is yet another potential problem with the use of emerging consensus. On certain issues, European states may be divided between several fundamentally different conceptions of what constitutes good policy. In these cases, the states' ranking of potential legal solutions may include second-best and third-best options that cannot be aggregated in a way that fulfills the elementary condition of transitivity. This problem was named the Condorcet Paradox, and it may prove real in complex questions such as the right of prisoners to vote. When faced with such problems, the ECHR may need to abandon the use of emerging consensus – which doesn't enjoy the same informational value it does in simpler issues involving a more binary set of options – and use other doctrines instead.

It seems intuitive to assume that a binding judgment of an international court is the final word on any policy matter. If this judgment obviates the need for a public debate and limits the engagement of people in politics, a serious problem arises. But often the judgment of an international court is not the final word on the matter. A better metaphor for the intervention of international courts is that of a dialogue with the public and its officials. International courts may cast an effect on the public debate, but they do not silence it. In fact, they often improve public deliberation, as Chapter 4 argues.

International courts provide arguments for an informed debate, based on rights instead of on naked power. They create a powerful myth that severe problems can be solved according to principles of justice and the rule of law, which gives people an incentive to get involved in politics. Many international courts also act as social hubs that give international lawyers training and ideas and let them meet each other – invigorating the legal debate.

Furthermore, the resistance of political bodies to international courts involves the public and requires action by a host of administrative bodies. This process may rejuvenate national bodies and national constituencies instead of enfeebling them. Scholars have already noted that hostile responses of states to international courts' judgments may constrain these courts' discretion ex ante.[3] This chapter will call attention to the potential benefits of such responses ex post.

Unlike previous chapters, Chapter 5 doesn't focus on the decisions of international courts or their ultimate outcomes. Instead, it addresses the process of decision making by international courts and the danger that this process will be captured by interest groups.

International courts do not work on their own initiative. They depend on applicants to bring cases for their decision. These applicants can sometimes be powerful and well-informed NGOs. At other times, NGOs may submit amicus curiae briefs as an attempt to influence the court's decision, or operate in the shadows by funding and providing legal advice to applicants. NGOs can help the court's interest by supplying it with information and with opportunities to decide cases. They can also assist international courts by shaping public opinion in their favor or by supporting them in international fora. Finally, they can help monitor compliance with the court's judgments. All these are advantages arising from the intervention of NGOs, but they also raise the concern of undue influence that these NGOs will exert on the court in return for the benefits they confer on it.

The concerns raised by the participation of NGOs in international courts' proceedings are real. They need to be addressed while taking into account the specific character of the court and the challenges it faces. The chapter suggests different procedures for different international courts based on their unique characteristics.

After an international court issues a judgment, the influence of NGOs doesn't end. NGOs may shame states into compliance by exposing their violations and creating potent reputational sanctions. The

[3] *See* Tom Ginsburg, *Bounded Discretion in International Judicial Lawmaking*, 45 VA. J. INT'L L. 631, 658 (2005); Jacob Katz Cogan, *Competition and Control in International Adjudication*, 48 VA. J. INT'L L. 411 (2008); SHAI DOTHAN, REPUTATION AND JUDICIAL TACTICS: A THEORY OF NATIONAL AND INTERNATIONAL COURTS, Cambridge University Press (2015).

question that remains is whether NGOs are likely to use these reputational sanctions in a biased way or in a way that is merited, considering the severity of state violations. Empirical research that I conducted regarding the submission of NGO reports to a new, publicly available, website operated by the Committee of Ministers – the body charged with enforcing judgments of the ECHR – suggests that international courts can create arenas where NGOs use accurate and beneficial reputational sanctions. By coding all the NGO reports filed on the website in the first four years of its existence, this research shows a focus of NGOs on the most severe violations and on the most important legal issues. The chapter explains this phenomenon using the tools of Social Network Analysis, an influential social science methodology. The research also shows that NGOs focus their shaming efforts on states that are usually well-behaving and spend less effort on states that regularly violate human rights. A series of quantitative tests and qualitative interviews with NGO lawyers and activists suggests that NGOs focus on well-behaving states because these NGOs believe well-behaving states are likely to improve their practices when facing criticism by the human rights community.

Chapter 6 moves on to the final challenge for the intervention of international courts in domestic affairs: the claim that this intervention eventually leads to worse outcomes all things considered. Domestic bodies and officers of the state operate under the shadow of potential judgments by international courts. This threat may give them the wrong incentives and make them act in ways that cause more harm than good. Partly to avert such a danger, many international courts voice a commitment to the principle of subsidiarity, a principle which relegates as many decisions as possible to the domestic level instead of the international level.

Subsidiarity is served by different doctrines in different courts. The ICC for example applies a rule of admissibility called complementarity, according to which it may not prosecute crimes that were prosecuted or investigated by national authorities. The existence of this rule gives states an incentive to investigate crimes committed by their soldiers in order to preempt ICC intervention. But the downside of complementarity is that it allows states to shield their soldiers from ICC prosecution by sham investigations that would not lead to a reasonable penalty.

It seems intuitive that the main justification to abandon the rule of complementarity in favor of a more interventionist rule – such as the rule of primacy adopted by the ad hoc criminal tribunals in Yugoslavia

(ICTY) and Rwanda (ICTR) – should be the existence of many states that are willing to conduct sham investigations. But the picture is a bit more complex. When the incentives of individual soldiers as well as those of state authorities are taken into account, a strategic analysis makes it clear that complementarity deters more soldiers than primacy as long as the probability of ICC prosecution is low. Only as the probability of prosecution increases over a certain threshold would a shift to primacy – either by treaty amendment or by judicial interpretation – improve deterrence.

It is possible to move the analysis one step backwards and assess what doctrines would make states more willing to subject themselves to the jurisdiction of international courts to begin with. The willingness of states to subject themselves to the ICC's jurisdiction depends on the rule of admissibility it applies and on the states' long-term goals. Similarly, other international courts may affect the willingness of states to join their jurisdiction or to increase their scope by the doctrines they develop. When the ECHR uses expansive interpretation, for example, it risks motivating states not to take on more obligations by approving any additional protocols. If states know that every obligation they agree to may be expanded by the court in ways they can't foresee, their natural response may be not to assume further obligations.

Chapter 7 concludes the book by providing a wider theoretical perspective on the intervention of international courts in domestic affairs. The chapter examines theories of domestic judicial review and shows the similarity between their insights and the analysis of international judicial review throughout the book. Naturally, the scholarship about judicial review by national courts is much more developed than the literature on international courts and can serve as a useful source of inspiration. Nevertheless, international courts have to face different circumstances than national courts, and the parallels between the ideas described in this book and theories of domestic judicial review are often quite complicated.

To account for the special conditions in which international courts operate, the chapter outlines the characteristics of the global arena today. The chapter describes a world with many centers of power connected to each other through numerous cross-cutting networks. These networks do not start at the top of each state's administrative hierarchy. Rather, they link mid-level government officials as well as private bodies and individuals in different states. International courts that operate in today's world cannot content themselves with assuring compliance to their judgments by states. They must address multiple audiences at the same time.

C Policy Implications

There is a fundamental difference between a book of this kind and a policy paper. A policy paper that wishes to direct action by administrators has to apply a cost-benefit analysis to specific factual situations. It has to balance numerous conflicting considerations that arise with regard to every set of facts and to quantify the effect of every one of these considerations. The book doesn't attempt this form of analysis.

Instead, the purpose of the book is to flesh out potential implications of the intervention of international courts in domestic affairs. It relies mainly on theoretical analysis but also on empirical investigations. The book engages in basic science – it tries to improve the scientific understanding of the world – not in applied science. It doesn't spell out direct policy recommendations for particular circumstances.

Nevertheless, the book certainly has normative implications and it attempts to make them as clear as possible in the chapters that follow. These implications are only arguments: arguments for or against judicial intervention in certain issues, or arguments in favor of giving states a certain degree of deference. In order to distill a policy recommendation from these arguments, the magnitude of harm or the potential advantage of judicial action would need to be assessed in light of specific facts. Other utilitarian considerations would inevitably have to be addressed at this point.

Chapter 2 doesn't attempt to assess the consequences of international judicial review, but rather tries to establish when it is normatively legitimate. Chapters 3 and 6 explain when doctrines of deference such as margin of appreciation or complementarity are likely to lead to the best outcomes. The analysis there is in a very high level of abstraction. It cannot direct judges exactly how to decide a concrete case, but it can guide them by exposing the hidden implications of the options at their disposal. Chapter 4 draws on a set of empirical findings to highlight some advantages of international judicial review. These advantages clearly have to be weighed against other potential disadvantages. Only Chapter 5 attempts to balance conflicting considerations regarding NGO intervention and to offer more concrete policy recommendations. But even these recommendations are quite general and would need to be adapted to the concrete needs of a certain court at a certain time.

The book attempts to demonstrate how actual judgments could be justified or explained as a method to achieve certain societal advantages. Some readers may find this practice to be Panglossian – as if I were arguing that international judges always live in the best of all possible worlds. But this isn't my intention. I do not argue that international courts always get it right. Rather, there are two reasons behind addressing specific judgments: to show what abstract principles would look like when materialized in the work of judges and to suggest that judges track these principles, consciously or unconsciously, at least some of the time.

Nowhere is it argued that judges always behave in ways that could be justified by the theory. On the contrary, by presenting an accurate picture of what good judicial practices look like, it is possible to criticize other judgments as digressing from these principles. The book therefore gives the reader tools to assess the quality of judicial decision making at international courts against a certain normative ideal.

Sometimes, judges may be aware of this ideal and deliberately try to reach it. But usually they would have only a basic intuition, an intuition which could be sharpened and significantly improved by the analysis in the book. For example, many judges probably share the intuition that by learning from the practices of the majority of countries in Europe according to the emerging consensus doctrine, they can discover good policies. But most judges – and most of the lawyers who read their judgments – probably didn't synthesize the conditions for optimizing the benefits of emerging consensus according to the Condorcet Jury Theorem. They didn't realize that by giving states a prior warning before a finding of violation, states can be encouraged to decide independently – fulfilling a pre-condition for the Jury Theorem to work. They may have never heard about the Condorcet Paradox, even if they had the intuition that some issues are too complicated for aggregating the views of different states.

By abstracting principles from judgments and carrying them to their ultimate logical ends, even the healthy instincts of experienced judges can be improved. Yet, as explained in this chapter, this book carries the reader only half of the way toward better judicial decisions. It presents the principles, but their application is always contingent on specific circumstances.

Furthermore, applying the ideas in this book to reality requires considering simultaneously the arguments made in several chapters. Every chapter of the book has a different focus, but they all come together to create a whole that is greater than its parts. Usually, several chapters would provide relevant perspectives for addressing the same factual situation. They would each provide arguments for or against judicial intervention in the same case.

Let's take a timely example: Imagine that you are an ECHR judge and you have to decide if a certain European country that disenfranchises all of its prisoners violates the European Convention on Human Rights. Chapter 2 would suggest that it is legitimate for you to intervene in a case like this, because the state cannot be trusted to represent the interests of its prisoners who cannot even vote. But even if judicial intervention is legitimate, it isn't necessarily recommended. You would have to consider whether you can set better policy than the state in that case. Chapter 3 suggests that the emerging consensus doctrine cannot provide you with epistemic superiority over domestic authorities because the policies of the states in Europe on the issue are too different to be aggregated.

This doesn't mean you shouldn't intervene, however. You should consider the fact that your intervention may enhance instead of stifling public deliberation, as Chapter 4 argues. You may even consider the beneficial effects of post-judgment shaming by the human rights community that are investigated in Chapter 5. These considerations may convince you that your intervention – even if it isn't guaranteed to hit on the best policy – may nevertheless lead to good consequences.

Then again, you can consider the effect of your present intervention on the future incentives of states to submit to further ECHR scrutiny by joining additional protocols. A similar issue is discussed, in a slightly different setting, in Chapter 6 regarding the incentives of states to join the ICC. The logic is quite simple: Even if your intervention would lead to good outcomes in the case at hand, it may drive away states from joining your court's jurisdiction in the future, something you wish to avoid. You may end up deciding not to intervene after all.

Being a judge, you would of course support your conclusion with references to doctrine and past judgments. There is nothing particularly strange or disingenuous about that. Other judges may have considered similar factors in the past, and you could easily choose the judgments and the doctrines that best suit the solution you have in mind.

After considering all the implications of your intervention on the world, you may even consider what effect it would have on your own court – whether it would lead to dangerous political backlash, for example. I have argued elsewhere that the practice of international, as well as national, courts is influenced by such egotistical considerations,[4] but they are not addressed in this book. This book is about how international courts can do good, not how they can do well.

[4] See Dothan, Note 3.

2

The Argument from Normative Legitimacy

Judges on international courts are not elected, but they bend the will of democratic countries. This poses a major challenge to the legitimacy of international courts.

Because international judges are not elected, they are not accountable to any public. They cannot be replaced if the public in countries under their jurisdiction thinks they are out of order. The concern here is not just with the quality of the court's judgments, but with the fact that the people do not get to choose the officials that affect their lives. In some courts, for example in the CJEU and the International Court of Justice (ICJ), judges have renewable terms, which gives the states under their jurisdiction some control over the judges.[1] Yet even this type of political control relies only on the decision of state representatives and not on a popular vote. Besides, in some courts, such as the ICC, judges who are selected for a full term cannot be re-selected.[2] The ECHR even shifted from renewable to nonrenewable terms.[3]

Although international courts do not have elected judges, many of them strive to have some representation of the countries under their jurisdiction. Often, this representation system is far from perfect. The ICJ, for example, has only fifteen judges that can hardly represent all the states under its jurisdiction, even if every judge comes from a different country as mandated by the ICJ statute.[4] To compensate, the statute allows states whose case is brought before the ICJ to elect judges who will

[1] Statute of the International Court of Justice, Art. 13(1); The Treaty on the Functioning of the European Union, Art. 253.

[2] Rome Statute of the International Criminal Court, Art. 36(9)(a)

[3] Convention for the Protection of Human Rights and Fundamental Freedoms as amended by Protocol No. 14, Art. 23(1) (presenting the current regime of non-renewable terms for judges); Protocol No. 11 to the Convention for the Protection of Human Rights and Fundamental Freedoms, Article 23(1) (presenting the old system of renewable terms).

[4] Statute of the International Court of Justice, Article 3(1).

sit specifically on this case.[5] A long tradition gives every permanent member of the Security Council the right to always have a judge on the court.[6]

The ECHR does manage to represent all countries under its jurisdiction by dictating that one judge would be selected in respect of every one of the forty-seven states of the Council of Europe.[7] In that case, the states are getting an equal representation, but individuals, the ultimate stakeholders, are grossly misrepresented. When San Marino and Liechtenstein – each with a population of less than 50,000 – have the same share of the court as Germany and the United Kingdom – with populations of well over 50 million each – the composition of the court in no way resembles the demographics of Europe.[8]

Judges on national courts are also not accountable to the public in many countries. This gives rise to the so-called counter-majoritarian difficulty – situations in which the actions of an accountable parliament are frustrated by nonaccountable judges. Yet the challenge that international courts are facing is greater than that directed at national courts. National judicial review is justified by a host of theories about checks and balances that are necessary within the state, because national courts protect basic human rights, or because they can help correct flaws in the democratic process. International courts, in contrast, intervene after all these mechanisms were already used. They do not just overrule the parliament; they contradict the decision of the state as a whole, after its national courts have reviewed the issue and all the domestic processes were brought to bear.

A series of power battles between international courts and states confirm that international courts do in fact routinely contradict the will of democracies. The United Kingdom didn't comply with the ECHR's judgment requiring it to give prisoners the right to vote,[9] and the United States was forced by its own Supreme Court to disobey a judgment of the

[5] *Id*, Art. 31.

[6] *See* www.icj-cij.org/court/?p1=1&p2=2.

[7] Convention for the Protection of Human Rights and Fundamental Freedoms, Art. 20, 22.

[8] *See* Lord Hoffmann, *The Universality of Human Rights*, Judicial Studies Board Annual Lecture, Mar. 19, 2009, available at https://conservativehome.blogs.com/files/hoffmann_2009_jsb_annual_lecture_universality_of_human_rights.pdf at par. 38 (suggesting this implies the ECHR lacks constitutional legitimacy).

[9] *See* Hirst v. *The* United Kingdom (No. 2), judgment of October 6, 2005, 2005-IX EUR. Ct. H.R. 187; Greens and MT v. United Kingdom, judgment of November 23, 2010, Reports of Judgments and Decisions 2010.

ICJ despite the willingness of the US President to comply.[10] States with long and illustrious democratic traditions are colliding with international courts and raise a real challenge to their legitimacy.

Perhaps one can argue that states deliberately put themselves in this position by agreeing to the jurisdiction of international courts. States wished to limit their future actions by committing to a certain set of provisions.[11] Certainly, state sovereignty also implies the ability to commit, but this would seem to bind states only to the things they actually agreed to. International courts are not only interpreting states' commitments restrictively. They are expanding their treaty obligations and changing them over time. Even if international courts do not ignore their founding texts, they cannot rely on state consent when they are going against the intentions of states.

The actual will of states when they accepted their treaty obligations should form a constraint on the court's discretion. So should the current practices of the state, to the extent that they do not contradict its own commitments. States should be allowed a margin of appreciation – their policies should be deferred to in recognition of their superior democratic credentials. But the deference given to the states should only go so far. The purpose of this chapter is to delineate the situations in which international courts are entitled to intervene as this challenge to their legitimacy is resolved.

A The Problem of Authority and the Meaning of State Consent

International courts are legal institutions tasked with fulfilling a set of goals that are mandated by states or international organizations.[12] As legal institutions, international courts are constrained by the treaties that create them. They cannot exceed the boundaries of the texts that are the basis of their authority. However, the treaties that establish international

[10] *See* Case Concerning Avena and Other Mexican Nationals (Mex. v. U.S.), [2004] ICJ Rep. 12; Medellin v. Texas, 552 U.S. 491 (2008).

[11] *See* Andrew Moravcsik, *The Origins of Human Rights Regimes: Democratic Delegation in Postwar Europe*, 54 INT'L ORG. 217 (2000). (arguing that states formed the ECHR deliberately to commit themselves to democratic principles against future political developments); Beth A. Simmons & Allison Danner, *Credible Commitments and the International Criminal Court*, 64 INT'L ORG. 225 (2010) (arguing that some states joined the ICC in order to commit not to engage in international crimes).

[12] *See* Yuval Shany, *Assessing the Effectiveness of International Courts: A Goal-Based Approach*, 106 AMER. J. INT'L. L. 225, 240–242 (2012).

courts are usually ambiguous texts that can be interpreted in several ways. While courts cannot contradict their founding texts, they can interpret them expansively. Expansive interpretation should be justified; if it digresses from the will of the state parties, it must serve another, higher goal.

1 *The Limits of the Treaty's Text*

The American Legal Realists investigated the inherent ambiguity of all legal texts. They pointed to three reasons that make legal texts amenable to several possible interpretations: (1) Legal texts are indeterminate because language is often unclear or ambivalent and because the authors of the text are unable to predict and address every future event; (2) the legal system usually contains many alternative and conflicting rules that apply to the same situation; (3) as the legal rule is applied to factual situations, the facts and the law are both inevitably adapted in a way that involves judicial discretion.[13] All these reasons apply to international treaties. If anything, they apply to them with greater force than they apply to domestic law.

The reason international law is more open to interpretation than domestic law is that the sources of international law do not come together to form one coherent system. International law is composed of legal provisions that are motivated by conflicting reasons. Therefore, even a single rule pertaining to a situation may be open to contradictory interpretations in light of the opposing reasons that motivate it.[14]

Some scholars argue that, despite all this, there are still clear cases in international law that do not involve any judicial discretion.[15] These cases are often termed "easy cases." They involve, for example, technical provisions that pertain to the structure of the court, provisions which cannot be avoided by interpretation.[16]

The existence and the prevalence of easy cases in international law could be debated. Yet even to the extent that there are easy cases, this doesn't imply that the judge is exempt from using any interpretation.

[13] *See* Hanoch Dagan, *The Realist Conception of Law*, 57 Uni. Toronto. L.J. 607, 613–616 (2007).

[14] Martti Koskenniemi, From Apology to Utopia: The Structure of International Legal Argument 590–591 (2005).

[15] Eirik Bjorge, The Evolutionary Interpretation of Treaties, 21–22 (2014).

[16] Consider the example of the number of permanent judges on the International Court of Justice (15, according to Art. 3(1) of the court's statute) discussed at *Id.*

A simple text still requires the use of interpretation, although this interpretation may be purely textual.[17] In fact, the textual method of treaty interpretation is an important judicial tool, and judges that are faced with clear texts are forced to use it.

If the court interprets a clear text using textual interpretation, it will be left with one interpretation that it cannot digress from. Such a digression will be considered an ultra vires act as it would undermine the very norm that authorizes the court.[18] Yet even if the judge is faced with a text that is unclear and the judge is forced to use other methods of interpretation to construe it, the text still forms a constraint on the judge's discretion. As judges interpret the text, they form a certain realm of possible readings that are all legitimate. Going beyond this realm would involve contradicting the text and acting without authority.[19]

2 *Restrictive Interpretation and Consent as a Standard*

After judges delineate the realm of potential interpretations of a treaty, they have to choose a single interpretation to set in their judgment. This choice involves judicial discretion, but that discretion is not unbounded. Judges are constrained to respect the principle of state consent. According to this principle, states are bound to respect obligations they took upon themselves and are not obligated to do anything they didn't commit to. This implies that the judges should usually follow the intentions of the state parties and should not impose on them obligations they didn't willingly assume.

[17] *See* Aharon Barak, Purposive Interpretation in Law 49–51 (2003) (Hebrew). Compare Ulf Linderfalk, *Is the Hierarchical Structure of Articles 31 and 32 of the Vienna Convention Real or Not? Interpreting the Rules of Interpretation*, 54 Netherlands Int'l L. Rev. 133, 141 (2007) (Explaining the so-called clear meaning doctrine in treaty interpretation. This doctrine, relying on the phrasing of article 33(4) to the Vienna Convention on the Law of Treaties, assumes that there are treaties which do not require any sort of interpretation. The normative implications of this contrast are limited, however, because one can use the word "interpretation" to refer only to the cognitive act of making sense of a text, without applying interpretative discretion or consulting external sources).

[18] *See* Rudolf Bernhardt, *Evolutive Treaty Interpretation, Especially of the European Convention on Human Rights* 42 German Y. B. Int'l L. 11, 24 (1999) (applying the unorthodox term "ultra vires" to the ECHR's treaty interpretation); *Cf.* Eyal Benvenisti, The Law of Global Governance 89–92 (2014) (discussing some problems of applying the ultra vires doctrine to international organizations).

[19] *See* Aharon Barak, Judicial Discretion 35–41 (1987) (Hebrew).

The court's commitment to the intentions of the parties is manifested in what is known as the "subjective approach" to treaty interpretation. This approach directs the court to consider, as the primary source of treaty interpretation, the intentions of the parties when they signed the treaty.[20] The commitment to the intention of the parties doesn't mean that the interpretation of the treaty cannot evolve, as the parties may have intended to match the provisions of the treaty to changing circumstances.[21] In fact, states often understand that they cannot foresee all the future circumstances surrounding their agreement and nonetheless want to cement their commitment to cooperate by forming a treaty that will be subjected to evolutionary interpretation.

The focus on the intentions of the parties also doesn't mean that the text of the treaty is redundant. The text of the treaty usually encapsulates the intention of the parties in the most precise way.[22] After all, the process of negotiating treaties is targeted at manifesting the intention of the parties as accurately as possible. This seems to imply that a restrictive interpretation of the text gives the greatest respect to the consent of the state parties. Restrictive interpretation is a choice made by the judges once several possible interpretations of the treaty are unveiled. At this stage, a restrictive interpretation would choose the interpretation that limits the states' obligations to the minimum.[23]

[20] *See* Francis G. Jacobs, *Varieties of Approach to Treaty Interpretation: With Special Reference to the Draft Convention on the Law of Treaties before the Vienna Diplomatic Conference*, 18 INT'L. & COMP. L.Q. 318, 319 (1969). Some may wonder if reference to the classical interpretive approaches is still needed after the Vienna Convention on the Law of Treaties created a comprehensive guide to treaty interpretation (see Notes 28–29; ALEXANDER ORAKHELASHVILI, THE INTERPRETATION OF ACTS AND RULES IN PUBLIC INTERNATIONAL LAW 309 (2008).) Nevertheless, this terminology is still useful in highlighting certain aspects of treaty interpretation, even if they are covered by articles 31–33 to the Vienna Convention.

[21] *See* BJORGE, Note 15 at 62–63 (suggesting that parties may harbor abstract and general intentions that should be adapted to changing circumstances and lead to evolving concrete meanings in the process of interpretation).

[22] *See* Malgosia Fitzmaurice & Panos Merkouris, *Canons of Treaty Interpretation: Selected Case Studies from the World Trade Organization and the North American Free Trade Agreement in* TREATY INTERPRETATION AND THE VIENNA CONVENTION ON THE LAW OF TREATIES: 30 YEARS ON 153, 156 (Malgosia Fitzmaurice et al., eds., 2010).

[23] *See* IVAN. A. SHEARER STARKE'S INTERNATIONAL LAW, 436–437 (11th ed., 1994).

Yet the principle of state consent is not a strict rule of interpretation. Instead, it is a standard that guides the judges to respect state's choices and state sovereignty. This respect is usually manifested in applying restrictive interpretation to the text, because it is the most accurate possible depiction of the will of the states.[24] The states, in turn, are usually the best possible representatives of all individuals affected by their actions. These individuals are the ultimate stakeholders – the true purpose of defending state sovereignty.[25] They are the ones that the court protects by restrictively interpreting the treaty.

Sometimes, however, a restrictive interpretation of the treaty's text doesn't optimally capture the will of states. Alternatively, the states themselves may misrepresent the individuals affected by their actions. These situations permit the court to use expansive interpretation, as the next sub-chapter argues.

B When Expansive Interpretation Is Legitimate

The use of expansive interpretation by international courts is anything but new. Scholars have noted that already the Permanent Court of International Justice (PCIJ), as well as its successor, the ICJ, have clearly opted for expansive interpretation and against restrictive interpretation of treaties.[26] Nevertheless, few courts have used expansive interpretation so openly and consistently as the ECHR, or incurred so much criticism and resistance for doing so. This, together with the fact that the ECHR is an incredibly prolific and influential international court that issued many thousands of judgments,[27] makes it the perfect case study for the analysis in this sub-chapter.

[24] Orakhelashvili, Note 20 at 413–415 (explaining that restricting a treaty to less than its text implies to defend state sovereignty is indefensible theoretically because it protects the sovereignty of some states at the expense of others).

[25] *See* Anne Peters, *Humanity as the A and Ω of. Sovereignty*, 20 Eur. J. Int'l L. 513, 514 (2009); Jeremy Waldron, *Are Sovereigns Entitled to the Benefit of the International Rule of Law*, 22 Eur. J. Int'l L. 315, 325–326 (2011).

[26] *See* Hersch Lauterpacht, *Restrictive Interpretation and the Principle of Effectiveness in the Interpretation of Treaties*, 26 Brit. Y.B. Int'l. L. 48, 51, 67 (1949). Orakhelashvili, Note 20 at 421–422 (suggesting that there are nevertheless some cases where international courts, including the ECHR, use restrictive interpretation without admitting it).

[27] *See* Erik Voeten, *The Politics of International Judicial Appointments: Evidence from the European Court of Human Rights*, 61 Int'l. Org. 669, 671 (2007) (discussing the importance and influence of the ECHR).

1 Expansive Interpretation in the ECHR

Treaty interpretation is regulated by the Vienna Convention on the Law of Treaties.[28] The relevant articles of the Vienna Convention are accepted as customary international law and were used by international courts long before 1980, when the convention came into effect.[29]

The provisions in the Vienna Convention are compatible with both expansive interpretation and restrictive interpretation. The International Law Commission, which drafted the convention, highlighted that if several interpretations of a treaty are possible, interpretations that do not give the treaty "appropriate effects" should be discarded since they do not interpret the treaty in good faith and in accordance with its object and purpose.[30] However, often this would leave a few legitimate interpretations, some of which require more from the state parties than others. An expansive interpretation would choose one of the interpretations that increases the obligations of the states.

The ECHR often refers to the so-called principle of effectiveness“ as justifying the use of expansive interpretation. But expansive interpretation doesn't just give the treaty appropriate effect. It chooses to give it a greater effect rather than a lesser effect.[31] Although the International Law Commission was committed to the idea that treaties should be construed as effective, it deliberately didn't mention the principle of effectiveness in the Vienna Convention from fear that this would lead to an overly expansive interpretation of treaties, which would contradict their letter and spirit.[32] The ECHR has used a large variety of interpretive techniques in the name of the principle of effectiveness that actually pushed forward an expansive interpretation of its founding document: The European Convention on Human Rights (Convention).[33]

[28] Vienna Convention on the Law of Treaties, 23 May 1969, 1155 UNTS 331, Arts. 31–33.

[29] *See* Herbert W. Briggs, *United States Ratification of the Vienna Treaty Convention*, 73 AMER. J. I. L. 470, 471–472 (1979); Case of Golder v. The United Kingdom judgment of February 21, 1975 EUR. Ct. H.R. (ser. A)18 at par. 29 (deciding that the ECHR will apply articles 31–33 of the Vienna Convention because they represent "generally accepted principles of international law" even before the treaty came into force).

[30] *Draft Articles on the Law of Treaties with Commentaries*, 2 YEARBOOK OF THE INTERNATIONAL LAW COMMISSION 187, 219 (1966).

[31] *See* Lauterpacht, Note 26 at 70, YORAM DINSTEIN, INTERNATIONAL TREATIES 133–135 (1974) (Hebrew).

[32] *Draft Articles on the Law of Treaties with Commentaries*, Note 30 at 219.

[33] Convention for the Protection of Human Rights and Fundamental Freedoms, Nov. 4, 1950, 213 U.N.T.S. 222. *See* P. VAN DIJK & G. J. H. VAN HOOF, THEORY AND PRACTICE OF THE EUROPEAN CONVENTION ON HUMAN RIGHTS 74–76 (3d ed., 1998). J. G.

The ECHR often stressed that the Convention is a law-making treaty – it sets norms and procedures to protect human rights within the Council of Europe. Because of its law-making nature, the ECHR ruled that the Convention should be interpreted in a way that makes its safeguards of human rights effective, not in a way that restricts state obligations.[34] While the International Law Commission made a deliberate choice not to differentiate between law-making treaties and treaties that resemble a contract, scholars have argued for special rules of interpretation to accommodate the unique nature of law-making treaties – treaties that should address changing conditions across long stretches of time.[35] The fact that the Convention is a law-making treaty may account for the need to adapt its provisions to evolving circumstances in order to give it proper effect. But the ECHR did much more than that. In numerous judgments, it made interpretive choices that expanded the obligations of states in the Council of Europe.

The ECHR adopted interpretations that further the protection of rights even when they contradict more formalistic interpretations. For example, in *Minelli* v. *Switzerland*, a journalist was prosecuted for defamation, but because a limitation period passed, this prosecution was repealed. The national court ordered the defendant to pay two-thirds of the court's costs, assuming he would have been convicted if it wasn't for the limitation period. Although the national court didn't issue a formal decision that the defendant was guilty, the ECHR found the national court's decision in violation of the presumption of innocence protected by article 6(2) of the Convention.[36]

The ECHR did more than transcend formal interpretations. It actually read into the Convention rights that do not appear in the text. For

MERRILLS, THE DEVELOPMENT OF INTERNATIONAL LAW BY THE EUROPEAN COURT OF HUMAN RIGHTS 98–124 (2d ed.,1993).

34 *See* Case of Wemhoff v. Germany judgment of June 27, 1968 EUR. Ct. H.R. (ser. A) 7 at 23; *Soering* case, judgment of July 7, 1989, EUR. Ct. H.R (ser. A)161 at 34. *See also* Case of Ireland v. The United Kingdom judgment of January 18, 1978 EUR. Ct. H.R. (ser. A) 25 at 90; Golder v. The United Kingdom, App. No. 4451/70, Eur. Comm'n H.R., (ser. B no. 16) June 1, 1973, par. 57; D. J. HARRIS, M. O'BOYLE & C. WARBRICK, LAW OF THE EUROPEAN CONVENTION ON HUMAN RIGHTS 7 (1995); F. Matscher, *Methods of Interpretation of the Convention*, in THE EUROPEAN SYSTEM FOR THE PROTECTION OF HUMAN RIGHTS 63, 66 (R. St. J. Macdonald, F. Matscher, & H. Petzold, eds., 1993).

35 *See Draft Articles on the Law of Treaties with Commentaries*, Note 30 at 219. Paul Mahoney, *Judicial Activism and Judicial Self-Restraint in the European Court of Human Rights: Two Sides of the Same Coin*, 11 HUM. R. L.J. 57, 64–65 (1990).

36 Minelli v. Switzerland, judgment of March 25, 1983, EUR. Ct. H.R. (ser. A)62.

example, in *Soering* v. *United Kingdom*, the ECHR decided that extraditing a person to the United States, where he might be detained for years awaiting a death sentence, violated article 3 of the Convention. This article forbids subjecting people "to torture or to inhuman or degrading treatment or punishment." It says nothing about extradition.[37]

Other ECHR judgments required states to provide practical safeguards that ensure the actual enjoyment of Convention rights. For example, in *Airey* v. *Ireland*, the ECHR ruled that article 6(1) of the Convention, defending the right to access national courts, was violated because the applicant couldn't afford to pay for a lawyer to represent her before the national court and wasn't able to do so properly herself.[38] In *Artico* v. *Italy*, the ECHR ruled that the right of a defendant in a criminal trial to receive free legal representation, guaranteed in article 6(3)(c) of the Convention, doesn't end when a lawyer is appointed for the defendant. The state is responsible to either assure that the lawyer represents the case properly or to replace him if necessary.[39]

The ECHR also read articles that are phrased as providing protection from state action as creating positive obligations on the state. For example, in *Marckx* v. *Belgium*, the ECHR decided that article 8 of the Convention, which protects the right to private and family life, requires the state to take positive measures to ensure that illegitimate children can lead a normal family life.[40]

The states were required by the ECHR to protect human rights from infringement by private parties. The case of *X and Y* v. *Netherlands* concerned a mentally handicapped adult who was raped, but her father was legally unable to file a complaint in her name. The court used that case to find the state in violation because its legal system didn't adequately protect the applicant from the actions of other individuals.[41]

ECHR judgments prevented states from evading responsibility by seeing through attempts to shift responsibility to other actors. In *Van der Mussele* v. *Belgium*, a lawyer was compelled by the local bar to represent defendants without any compensation. Even though the state didn't directly order the applicant to do anything, it did force the bar to

[37] Soering v. United Kingdom, judgment of July 7, 1989, EUR. Ct. H.R (ser. A)161.
[38] Airey v. Ireland, judgment of October 9, 1979, EUR. Ct. H.R. (ser. A)32.
[39] Artico v. Italy, judgment of May 13, 1980 EUR. Ct. H.R. (ser. A)37.
[40] Marckx v. Belgium, Judgment of June 13, 1979 EUR. Ct. H.R. (ser. A)31.
[41] X and Y v. The Netherlands, Judgment of March 26,1985 EUR. Ct. H.R. (ser. A)91.

make the bar's members represent clients without compensation and was found to be just as responsible as if it acted directly.[42]

In addition, the ECHR narrowly interpreted the exceptions and the derogations mentioned in the Convention.[43] It also gave a narrow interpretation to state reservations.[44]

The ECHR also expanded its ability to constrain state behavior by procedural decisions. The court relaxed the condition that applicants must be victims[45] and allowed relatives of a deceased victim to bring a case concerning a violation of the right to life.[46] In *CLR* v. *Romania*, the ECHR decided that a NGO can represent a child of Roma descent who died of mal-treatment, even though this organization is formally unable to serve as the attorney of the deceased and the application was lodged only after his death.[47]

After some back-and-forth in its judgments,[48] the ECHR clearly decided to apply its jurisdiction to territories outside the borders of member states. In *Al-Skeini v. United Kingdom*, the ECHR found the United Kingdom violated article 2, protecting the right to life, because it failed to properly investigate the killing of civilians by British forces in

[42] Van der Mussele v. Belgium, judgment of November 23, 1983 EUR. Ct. H.R. (ser. A)70 at 15

[43] Case of *Klass and others* Judgment of September 6, 1978 EUR. Ct. H.R. (ser. A)28 at 21; MERRILLS, Note 33 at 116.

[44] MERRILLS, Note 33 at 116–119.

[45] VAN DIJK & VAN HOOF, Note 33 at 76.

[46] See Fairfield and Others v. The United Kingdom, Decision of March 8, 2005.

[47] CLR v. Romania, judgment of July 17, 2014, Reports of Judgments and Decisions EUR. Ct. H.R. 2014.

[48] Bankovic and Others v. Belgium and Others, Decision of December 12, 2001, EUR. Ct. H.R. 2001-XII 333 is a decision that limits the court's jurisdiction for actions taken out of the territory of all members states in the Council of Europe, in that case, the bombing by NATO forces in the former Yugoslavia. Some criticized this judgment as digressing from previous decisions to apply extraterritorial jurisdiction to territories in Cyprus that were under the effective control of Turkey, *see* Case of Loizidou v. Turkey (Preliminary Objections) Judgment of March 23, 1995, EUR. Ct. H.R. (ser.A) 310 at pp. 23–24 par. 62, Case of Loizidou v. Turkey, judgment of December 18, 1996 (merits) *Reports of Judgments and Decisions* 1996-VI at pages 2234–2235 par. 52. The court's judgments can, with some difficulty, be reconciled if one considers that Yugoslavia was never under the court's jurisdiction while Cyprus was under its jurisdiction before falling under Turkey's occupation, *see* Alexandra Ruth and Mirja Trilsch, Bankovic v. Belgium *(Admissibility)*, 97 AM. J. INT'L L 168, 172 (2003). In any case, the court clearly chose the expansive view of extra-territoriality, applying it even to territories out of Europe, in Al-Skeini and Al-Jedda.

occupied Iraq.[49] In *Al-Jedda v. United Kingdom* – issued on the same day as *Al-Skeini* – the ECHR found the United Kingdom in violation of article 5 of the Convention, which protects the right to liberty, because it detained a British and Iraqi citizen in British-occupied Iraq.[50]

In a series of other judgments, the ECHR acquired another powerful tool in its legal arsenal. It started to issue judgments that require states to take specifically dictated actions, instead of allowing them to choose the means of remedying the violation declared by the court. These cases are known as "Pilot Judgments."[51]

This entire process was gradual. It increased the obligations required from the states over time.[52] In fact, the ECHR clearly championed a method of so-called evolutionary interpretation that was used to adjust the Convention to changing conditions and usually resulted in incrementally improving the protection of human rights.[53]

The interpretive techniques described previously inclined the ECHR toward the use of teleological interpretation.[54] Teleological interpretation is flexible enough to interpret the rights of individuals expansively and the limitations on these rights restrictively. This flexibility also allows teleological interpretation to shift the meaning of the Convention over time.[55]

But this flexibility that the court attained and its use to expand the obligations of democratic states may conflict with the principle of state consent. It can only be defended if there is good reason to believe that the Convention, interpreted restrictively, doesn't adequately represent the interests of all European states, or of the people residing in these states. These two possibilities are explored in the next two sub-chapters.

[49] Al-Skeini and others v. The United Kingdom, Judgment of July 7, 2011, Reports of Judgments and Decisions EUR. Ct. H.R. 2011.

[50] Al-Jedda v. The United Kingdom, Judgment of July 7, 2011, Reports of Judgments and Decisions EUR. Ct. H.R. 2011.

[51] See Broniowski v. Poland, judgment of June 22, 2004, 2004-V EUR. Ct. H.R. 1.

[52] *See* Shai Dothan, *Judicial Tactics in the European Court of Human Rights*, 12 CHI. J. INT'L. L. 115 (2011). DOTHAN, Note 3, Chapter 1.

[53] *See Tyrer* case, judgment of April 25, 1978 EUR. Ct. H.R. (ser. A) 26, at 15–16.

[54] *See* François OST, *The Original Canons of Interpretation of the European Court of Human Rights*, *in* THE EUROPEAN CONVENTION FOR THE PROTECTION OF HUMAN RIGHTS: INTERNATIONAL PROTECTION VERSUS NATIONAL RESTRICTIONS 283, 292 (Mireille Delmas-Marty, ed., 1992).

[55] Dothan, Note 52 at 131. *See also* DINSTEIN, Note 31 at 133 (connecting teleological interpretation and the principle of effectiveness).

2 *When Treaties Do Not Represent the Will of States*

Treaties are born of negotiations between countries. The rules that regulate the creation of treaties, listed in the Vienna Convention, are meant to ensure that the treaty will reflect the will of the states that joined it. However, while these rules prevent clear cases of coercion or fraud in treaty negotiations,[56] they do not prevent states from using other methods of extortion. These methods do not render the treaty illegitimate, but they should reflect on its interpretation.

As states negotiate a treaty, some states need the treaty more than others. States who need the treaty least have a credible threat to leave the negotiations table. They can use this threat to limit the obligations of the treaty far more than the other parties wish. A historical example is the pressure exerted by the United Kingdom on the other parties to the Convention. This pressure resulted in a weak and incomplete document, against the wishes of most parties.[57]

Lawmaking treaties are often joined by many states that did not take part in their negotiation. These parties are unable to change the text of the treaty and assume more obligations desirable for them. As years pass, conditions may change and even the original parties of the treaty may wish to change or increase their obligations. But an amendment to the treaty often requires the agreement of all signatories, giving each and every one of them a veto power against such amendment. States may use their veto power strategically to extract concessions from other countries. Russia, for example, refused to accept Protocol 14 to the Convention for years because of what it viewed as political judgments by the ECHR.[58] Protocol 14 was necessary to allow the ECHR to face modern conditions. All European states besides Russia ratified it years before Russia finally agreed to do so.[59] Their will was frustrated due to the Russian veto.

[56] *See* Vienna Convention on the Law of Treaties, Arts. 48–52.

[57] *See* Ed Bates, The Evolution of the European Convention on Human Rights – From Its Inception to the Creation of a Permanent Court of Human Rights 92–93, 95, 100 (2010).

[58] Russian President Vladimir Putin said that the Russian State Duma (lower house of parliament) considered the political decisions of the ECHR when it decided not to approve Protocol 14, *see* Bill Bowring, The Degradation of the International Legal Order? The Rehabilitation of Law and the Possibility of Politics 97 (2008).

[59] Russia eventually approved the ratification of Protocol 14 only in 2010, *see* https://wcd.coe.int/ViewDoc.jsp?p=&id=1571749&Site=DC&BackColorInternet=F5CA75&BackColorIntranet=F5CA75&BackColorLogged=A9BACE&direct=true.

All this isn't to say that states do not have a right to resist incurring obligations they didn't willingly assume or that they cannot legitimately resist such obligations for ulterior motives. A court that interprets the treaty cannot change the text or ignore it. It cannot impose on the states obligations that have no bearing in the text. But it can use expansive interpretation.

Expansive interpretation is legitimate when there is reason to believe that the treaty doesn't reflect the will of all its parties. When most parties would have preferred to incur greater obligations than a restrictive interpretation of the treaty implies, a restrictive interpretation doesn't do justice to the will of the parties. In these cases, courts should be allowed to use expansive interpretation.

3 *States that Misrepresent Their Public*

States are sometimes pre-empted from assuming obligations they are interested in because of the resistance of other states. Yet at other times this constraint doesn't apply, and the wish of the states not to undertake a specific obligation is evident. An example for a clear choice against assuming obligations is the decision of a state not to join an additional protocol.

The Convention allows European states to assume further obligations by creating and ratifying additional Protocols. Unlike amending protocols, additional protocols do not change the Convention itself. They only add new obligations on the states that ratified them, functioning essentially as separate treaties.[60] States usually agree that an additional protocol will become effective when a certain number of states ratified it. Other states can then join the Protocol by ratification and become immediately bound by it. From that point on, every state that decides not to join the protocol makes a conscious decision not to accept the obligations that this protocol entails.

This didn't stop the ECHR from subjecting states that didn't sign an additional protocol to the obligations contained in it. A clear example of that is the expansive interpretation of article 14 – protecting individuals against discrimination in the enjoyment of their Convention rights – to include discriminative practices that do not fall within the ambit of another Convention right.

[60] Donna Gomien, David Harris & Leo Zwaak, Law and Practice of the European Convention on Human Rights and the European Social Charter, 18 (1996).

On the face of it, article 14 is clear: it protects against discrimination in the enjoyment of the rights and freedoms set in the Convention. It doesn't form a general right against discrimination of interests and rights not mentioned in the Convention.[61] In the *Belgian Linguistic case*, the ECHR stressed that article 14 doesn't have an independent existence from other Convention articles. However, this judgment stressed that even infringements of other Convention rights that – taken independently – fall within the state's legitimate discretion and do not constitute a violation may be considered as a violation when this article is taken in conjunction with article 14.[62] Later ECHR judgments reiterated that only violations falling within the ambit of another Convention article can be considered a violation of article 14.[63]

Some states in Europe thought that this limited protection against discrimination isn't enough. They decided to draft an additional protocol, Protocol 12, which would protect against discrimination in the enjoyment of any right granted by national law, whether this right is protected by the Convention or not.[64] The protocol was open to signature in 2000. In April 2005, after the first ten states ratified it, the protocol entered into force. Therefore, since April 2005 every state that wants to increase its obligations to forbid discrimination in the protection of rights not mentioned in the Convention only has to ratify Protocol 12. Such a state isn't subject to any strategic behavior preventing it from willingly expanding its obligations.

Yet all that didn't stop the ECHR from expanding the obligations it imposed on the United Kingdom, which didn't ratify protocol 12, thereby clearly contradicting its independent choice. This expansion was done in the *Stec case*, which dealt with a pension regime that allegedly discriminated between men and women. The ECHR's admissibility decision held that social security payments are protected by article 1 of protocol 1 of the Convention – which protects the right to property – whether they are

61 *See* Case of Haas v. The Netherlands, judgment of January 13, 2004, Reports of Judgments and Decisions 2004-I at par. 41; Clare Ovey & Robin C.A. White, Jacobs & White The European Convention on Human Rights 413 (4th ed., 2006).

62 Case "relating to certain aspects of the laws on the use of languages in education in Belgium" judgment of July 23, 1968 EUR. Ct. H.R. (ser. A) 6 at 33–35. *See* Ovey & White, Note 61 at 415.

63 *See* Case of Abdulaziz, Cabales and Balkandali v. The United Kingdom, judgment of May 28, 1985 EUR. Ct. H.R. (ser. A) 94, par. 71.

64 *See* article 1 of Protocol 12 and the Explanatory Report on protocol 12, available at http://conventions.coe.int/Treaty/EN/Reports/Html/177.htm, par. 21–22.

funded by general taxation or by the beneficiaries.[65] This interpretation greatly expanded the ambit of the right to property and allowed the court to examine whether discrimination in pension rights violated article 14. Finally, the *Stec case* didn't find a violation of article 14,[66] but the expansion of the right to property meant in practice that certain social rights are protected from discrimination even if they are not mentioned in the Convention.

Judge Borrego Borrego wrote a concurring opinion in *Stec* that criticized the court's willingness to disregard the choice of states not to join protocol 12 by effectively imposing on all states a general right to equality with regard to social rights.[67] This isn't even an isolated case; the ECHR has consistently expanded the application of article 14 to social rights.[68]

Is Judge Borrego right? How can the court justify a direct contradiction to the will of a state not to expand its obligations? The principle of state consent seems to suggest that the obligations states took upon themselves should be interpreted restrictively. Yet the principle of state consent itself is justified by higher order principles. It is justified by the assumption that states are usually the best representatives of all individuals affected by their actions. The welfare and choices of these individuals are the ultimate goal that international courts serve.[69] When there is good reason to believe that states do not represent the interests of these individuals, the principle of state consent should not be adhered to – permitting the use of expansive interpretation.

This doesn't mean that international courts should pry open the state and monitor the democratic process within it. It only means that under some conditions democratic processes are suspect as they can easily fall prey to democratic failures. When faced with such situations, the assumption that states act in the best interests of everyone affected by their actions should be replaced by an assumption that judicial intervention is needed.

[65] Grand Chamber Decision as to the Admissibility of Applications nos. 65731/01 and 65900/01 by Stec and Others v. The United Kingdom, par. 53–56.

[66] Case of Stec and Others v. The United Kingdom, judgment of April 12, 2006, Reports of Judgments and Decisions 2006-VI.

[67] *Id.*

[68] *See* Rory O'Connell, *Cinderella Comes to the Ball: Art 14 and the Right to Non-discrimination in the ECHR*, 29 Leg. Stud. 211, 216 (2009).

[69] *See* Note 25; Armin von Bogdandy & Ingo Venzke, In Whose Name? A Public Law Theory of International Adjudication, 210–213 (2014).

The most obvious condition under which individuals are not adequately represented by their state occurs when people who can't vote are affected by state policies. Most of the human rights policies of democratic countries affect their own citizens, that is, people who take part in making the decisions that shape their fate. There are relatively few cross-national effects, so-called externalities, in human rights policies, in contrast with other areas of international law. This fact usually militates in favor of deference to the decisions states make regarding human rights.[70] But sometimes the most vulnerable individuals subject to state power are completely excluded from the democratic process.

Foreigners who live as aliens in countries that are not their own are usually unable to vote. Yet their wellbeing greatly depends on the authorities in their country of residence. This country can abuse their rights or deport them, putting them in a position that is usually much worse than that of citizens who hold the right to vote.[71] The ECHR cannot rely on the democratic process to protect the rights of those who are excluded from it. The court must use expansive interpretation to protect their rights.

To answer this challenge, the ECHR issued many judgments that protected the rights of aliens, sometimes against fierce state criticism. A famous example is the case of *Othman Abu Qatada* v. *United Kingdom*,[72] in which the court prevented the deportation of an extremist Muslim cleric to Jordan where he was supposed to stand trial for terrorism. The court stressed that the trial may rely on the confessions of third parties who were tortured. This decision delayed the deportation of Abu Qatada – who was eventually extradited after a legal struggle of eight years – and led to great disapproval in the United Kingdom.[73]

Another example is the *A. A.* v. *United Kingdom*[74] judgment that prevented the deportation of a Nigerian who was convicted of rape when he was fifteen years old. The court prevented the deportation because the applicant developed certain social ties in the United Kingdom. This

70 *See* Yuval Shany, *Toward a General Margin of Appreciation Doctrine in International Law?* 16 Eur. J. Int'l L. 907, 920 (2006).

71 *See* John Hart Ely, Democracy and Distrust – A Theory of Judicial Review 161 (1980)

72 Case of Othman (Abu Qatada) v. The United Kingdom, judgment of January 17, 2012, Reports of Judgments and Decisions 2012.

73 Erik Voeten, *Public Opinion and the Legitimacy of International Courts*, 14 Theo. Inq. L. 411, 418 (2013).

74 Case of A. A. v. The United Kingdom, judgment of September 20, 2011.

judgment constitutes an expansive reading of the right to private life to include not only family connections but also social ties more generally. The British press didn't mince words when reviewing the decision, calling it, among other things, "utterly perverse and sickening."[75]

But all this is nothing compared to the backlash the court suffered when it tried to protect another group that was excluded from the political process in the United Kingdom: prisoners. In several countries in Europe, prisoners are disenfranchised, either generally or under certain conditions. The ECHR decided in *Hirst* v. *United Kingdom* that the indiscriminate ban on prisoners' right to vote violates the Convention. Five years later, in *Greens and MT* v. *United Kingdom*, the ECHR specifically required the United Kingdom to amend its laws on the issue within six months. These judgments were not complied with. They led to harsh criticism in the United Kingdom with statements such as that of the British Prime Minister David Cameron, who said that giving the right to vote to anyone in prison makes him "physically ill."[76]

Foreigners and, in some countries, prisoners cannot vote at all. In contrast, democratic countries grant any other adult person exactly one vote. The problem is that one vote at the ballot often translates to more or less political power depending on the social group of the voter. So-called discrete and insular minorities are groups that are subject to prejudice – for example, because of their ethnicity, their religion, or their race. This prejudice prevents them from forming coalitions with other parties and social groups, effectively blocking them from taking over the government. The result, noted in the famous "footnote four" of the US Supreme Court judgment, *Carolene Products*,[77] is that the interests of this specific kind of minority are not fully represented by the regular democratic process.

The task of protecting minorities initially falls on the shoulders of national courts. These courts should make sure that everyone in society, even minorities, gets exactly the same rights. If nobody can be discriminated against, even minorities that are practically excluded from the democratic process are granted some form of "virtual

[75] James Slack, *Social Ties Keep Rapists in Britain*, Mail On Line Sept. 21, 2011, available at www.dailymail.co.uk/debate/article-2039657/Akindoyin-Akinshipe-Social-ties-rapists-Britain.html.

[76] *See* Andrew Hough, *Prisoner Vote: What MPs Said in Heated Debate*, The Telegraph Feb. 11, 2011, available at: www.telegraph.co.uk/news/politics/8317485/Prisoner-vote-what-MPs-said-in-heated-debate.html.

[77] United States v. Carolene Products Co., 304 U.S. 144 (1938).

representation." Virtual representation implies that the minority's rights are always tied to those of the majority, forcing the majority to represent the minority's interests as they strive to protect their own.[78]

When national courts fail to equalize the rights of all social groups, one can say that the state does not fully represent certain minorities. This gives the ECHR justification to intervene and protect the rights of discriminated minorities using expansive interpretation.[79] An example of the ECHR doing exactly that is the case of *DH and Others* v. *the Czech Republic.*

This case confronted the court with evidence that Roma children are significantly more likely to be sent to special schools where they are taught an inferior curriculum. The evidence by itself doesn't prove an intention to discriminate against the Roma. Instead, it qualifies as what the ECHR termed "indirect discrimination" – applying seemingly neutral criteria to all, which effectively put some in a better position than others. Usually, the ECHR would grant such policies a margin of appreciation and will not intervene. Intervention implies that the court would have to rely on factual evidence and review the state's policies in a way that would limit the state's legitimate discretion.[80] In the Chamber judgment of the court in this case, it refused to encroach on the state's discretion and decided discrimination cannot be proven.[81]

The applicants requested that the case be referred to the Grand Chamber, which overruled the Chamber's judgment. The Grand Chamber decided that indirect discrimination can violate the Convention. There is no need to prove intent. Statistical evidence that shows Roma children are disproportionally allocated to bad schools was enough to find a violation of article 14 – protecting against discrimination – taken in conjunction with article 2 of protocol 2, which protects the right to education.[82]

The Grand Chamber judgment stressed that the Roma are a "disadvantaged and vulnerable minority," which requires the ECHR to grant

[78] *See* Ely, Note 71 at 76–84, 151.

[79] *See* Eyal Benvenisti, *Margin of Appreciation, Consensus and Universal Standards*, 31 NYU J. INT'L L. POL. 843, 849 (1999) (arguing, based on this argument, that the ECHR should not grant a margin of appreciation to states that infringe the rights of minorities when the national judiciary doesn't guarantee their rights).

[80] *See* O'Connell, Note 68 at 220.

[81] Case of D.H. and Others v. The Czech Republic, judgment of February 7, 2006, par. 52–53.

[82] Case of D.H. and Others v. The Czech Republic, judgment of November 11, 2011, Reports of Judgments and Decisions 2007-IV, at par. 184.

them special protection.[83] Furthermore, the court's intervention is justified by the fact that the state didn't grant the necessary safeguards for the rights of the Roma as a minority group.[84] This implies that the ECHR considers the political weakness of the Roma, who are a typical discrete and insular minority, as a justification for its use of expansive interpretation. When the state fails to represent its minorities and discriminates against them, it falls to the court to protect their rights.

While small and distinct social groups are sometimes vulnerable minorities, at other times they may possess special political power over the rest of society.[85] Small groups can more easily prevent free-riding among their members than bigger groups, because each member of the group gains enough from cooperation to have an incentive to enforce it on all the other members.[86] Small groups can more easily monitor their members and coordinate their voting. They can also spread information about the behavior of politicians among the entire group, allowing them to discipline their representatives.[87] Sometimes small groups can threaten to leave the state's jurisdiction and take their business elsewhere, which gives them additional leverage against the government.[88]

For all these reasons, small interest groups can sometimes shape a state's treaty obligations to suit their own interests. This puts the rest of society at a disadvantage, constituting a potential democratic failure. The ECHR can use expansive interpretation when it suspects such a democratic failure occurs. An example of that is actually the *Stec case* itself – the judgment that provoked Judge Borrego's attack on expansive interpretation. *Stec* decided that social security benefits are protected by article 14 of the Convention. Such benefits concern the great bulk of the population: employees who find it difficult to organize and exercise effective political power. The state sometimes misrepresents these people because it is captured by small interest groups, such as large-scale

[83] *See id* at par. 181–182.

[84] *See id* at par. 207.

[85] *See* Bruce A. Ackerman, *Beyond Carolene Products*, 98 Harv. L. Rev. 713, 724 (1985); *See* Eyal Benvenisti, *Judicial Review and Democratic Failures: Minimizing Asymmetric Information through Adjudication*, 32 Tel. Aviv. Uni. L. Rev. 277, 280 (Hebrew). Eyal Benvenisti, *Exit and Voice in the Age of Globalization*, 98 Mich. L. Rev. 167, 170–175 (1999).

[86] *See* Mancur Olson, The Logic of Collective Action 33–34 (1965).

[87] *See* Susanne Lohmann, *An Information Rationale for the Power of Special Interests*, 92 Amer. Pol. Sci. Rev. 809, 812 (1998).

[88] *See* Albert O. Hirschman, Exit, Voice, and Loyalty – Responses to Decline in Firms, Organizations, and States 55 (1970).

employers and business tycoons. This legitimizes the use of expansive interpretation by the ECHR.

C The Proper Bounds of the Margin of Appreciation

When the ECHR reviews the policies of states, it is not constrained only by the text of the Convention. The court has also committed itself repeatedly to the doctrine of the margin of appreciation.[89] According to this doctrine, the ECHR grants states some latitude in interpreting their Convention obligations and defers to some of the states' policies even when these policies infringe human rights.

A potential justification for the margin of appreciation granted to the states relies on the ability of democracies to represent their citizens. If state policies are reached by a democratic process, it seems illegitimate that an international court that is not elected or accountable to the public overrule these policies.[90]

The margin of appreciation is not granted to the decision of the states to undertake treaty obligations. It is granted to policies that states adopt on their own, without interacting with other states. Nevertheless, to the extent that democratic failures plague the policy decisions of states, the ECHR is justified in denying any deference to state decisions.

In fact, scholars argued that the ECHR should not grant states a margin of appreciation in cases of potential democratic failures.[91] Others have argued that the ECHR judgments actually reflect this understanding and apply stricter scrutiny to cases in which states do not properly represent their citizens.[92]

The upshot of this analysis is that the ECHR should apply a narrower margin of appreciation in cases that are notorious for the possibility of democratic failures: foreigners and disenfranchised individuals,

89 *See* Case of Dickson v. The United Kingdom, judgment of December 4, 2007, at par. 77–78 (reiterating the ECHR's commitment to the margin of appreciation doctrine and explaining its boundaries).

90 *See* Shany, Note 70 at 919–921.

91 *See* Benvenisti, Note 79 at 849.

92 Andrew Legg, The Margin of Appreciation in International Human Rights Law: Deference and Proportionality 27–31 (2012). Andreas von Staden, *The Democratic Legitimacy of Judicial Review beyond the State: Normative Subsidiarity and Judicial Standards of Review*, 10 Int'l J. Con. L. 1023, 1042 (2012). Oddný Mjöll Arnardóttir, *The Differences that Make a Difference: Recent Developments on the Discrimination Grounds and the Margin of Appreciation under Article 14 of the European Convention on Human Rights*, 14 Hum. Rts. L. Rev. 647, 664–665 (2014).

vulnerable minorities, and groups rendered politically powerless by their inability to organize. These groups deserve a greater protection than the one usually granted to them by the state.

There is a more general argument here: International courts that face states with potential democratic failures should not defer to their policies. When the Inter-American Court of Human Rights (IACHR) started to function, to take an extreme example, it was faced with some countries that were still military dictatorships. The policies made by these countries possessed no democratic legitimacy and didn't deserve any deference. Scholars have argued that the IACHR took this into account when it bravely decided not to defer to these countries' policies.[93] Functioning democracies, in contrast, usually represent their citizens well, but known democratic failures are exceptions to this rule.

Because the international court cannot always observe the actual political processes in the state, surely mistakes will happen. There will be cases of suspected democratic failure where the victims actually had a significant voice in the determination of policy. There will also be policies that receive a margin of appreciation because no classic democratic failure was observed, even though the victims of these policies were actually politically helpless. It would be great if the ECHR could assess the actual political power of various groups. Sometimes it may even be able to do so.[94] In the main, though, political processes are complex and opaque. The ECHR has to regulate its policies by a set of rules that inevitably lead to some false positives and some false negatives.

D Conclusion

International courts like the ECHR make policy decisions that shape the lives of millions. Within the range of possibilities delimited by the law,

[93] *See* Gonzalo Candia, *Comparing Diverse Approaches to the Margin of Appreciation: The Case of the European and the Inter-American Court of Human Rights*, available at: http://papers.ssrn.com/sol3/papers.cfm?abstract_id=2406705 at p. 22.

[94] In fact, scholars have argued that the ECHR increasingly does something similar: It observes the domestic decision-making process in states under its jurisdiction and grants a wider margin of appreciation when this process is more commendable. *See* Robert Spano, *Universality or Diversity of Human Rights: Strasburg in the Age of Subsidiarity*, 14 Hum. Rts. L. Rev. 487, 498–499 (2014); Mikael Rask Madsen, *Rebalancing European Human Rights: Has the Brighton Declaration Engendered a New Deal on Human Rights in Europe*, 9 J. Int'l Dispute Settlement 199 203, 214 (2018). Oddný Mjöll Arnardóttir, *The Brighton Aftermath and the Changing Role of the European Court of Human Rights*, 9 J. Int'l Dispute Settlement 223, 234 (2018).

there is plenty of room to make choices. It is important that courts make the right choices, which can improve the welfare and the success of everyone involved. The next chapter argues international courts are often uniquely positioned to make the right choice. In contrast, the chapter concluded here offers a different argument.

The gist of the argument presented in this chapter is that international courts must strive to issue decisions that are normatively legitimate. Before the judges ask themselves if they are positioned to give a good decision, they should ask themselves if they should be the ones to decide. If the text of the treaty adequately reflects all the interests involved, the court should stick to it. If the policies of the state in question represent the will of all individuals, international courts should defer.

In contrast, when the court has reason to believe that the obligations states took upon themselves and the policies they adopted do not represent the will of all individuals, it can legitimately intervene. In these cases, the court can legitimately use expansive interpretation and narrow the margin of appreciation granted to the states. But this doesn't mean that the court should always do that.

Courts that intervene aggressively sometimes make bad policies. The margin of appreciation can be used not only to ensure the court defers to bodies with better democratic credentials. It can also be used to protect policies that are likely to suffer from judicial intervention instead of being improved by it. The next chapter offers plenty of examples of such cases.

There is yet another thing international courts have to consider. Even if they can improve on the policy of a state in a specific case and can do so legitimately, their decision may have harmful repercussions. States may be afraid of giving international courts more power if this is a power they cannot control. If the court expansively interprets its mandate to intervene in state policies, states may restrict this mandate.

This may be the reason why the United Kingdom didn't ratify Protocol 12 to the Convention. Protocol 12 allows the ECHR to find a violation in every discriminative allocation of rights granted by law, instead of limiting discrimination claims only to rights protected by the Convention itself. The chapter suggests that the ECHR effectively applied this stricter standard even to states that didn't ratify Protocol 12. The United Kingdom may have viewed this expansive interpretation as dangerous and unpredictable.

In a response of the British government to the British Parliament Joint Committee on Human Rights, the government suggested that one of the reasons it didn't join Protocol 12 is because it couldn't be sure this protocol would not be interpreted as applying the right to equality also to rights protected by other international human rights instruments the United Kingdom has joined. The commentary to Protocol 12 specifically explains that it would not apply to obligations under other international instruments,[95] but the British government suspected that with expansive interpretation the ECHR could bypass that limitation. The government decided it is better to wait and see how the judgments of the ECHR develop before granting it even more power.[96]

This example demonstrates that when courts use expansive interpretation they may give states an incentive to limit their treaty obligations to avoid even more intrusive judicial intervention. Successful courts must respond to this challenge, just like they respond to a host of other state countermeasures such as noncompliance, criticism, and budget cuts. Courts need not do everything that they can do legitimately. Sometimes they have to play it smart.[97]

[95] See Explanatory Report to the Protocol No. 12 to the Convention for the Protection of Human Rights and Fundamental Freedoms, available at https://rm.coe.int/CoERMPublicCommonSearchServices/DisplayDCTMContent?documentId=09000016800cce48, at par. 29.

[96] *See* www.publications.parliament.uk/pa/jt200405/jtselect/jtrights/99/9906.htm par. 31–32.

[97] I investigated the way courts do that in DOTHAN, Note 3, Chapter 1.

3

The Argument from Systemic Epistemic Superiority

Even if international courts can legitimately intervene in domestic affairs, there is no justification for intervention that leads to worse outcomes than states can reach on their own. International judges are not necessarily better than national judges and national politicians. If anything, the opposite may be the case. International judges are often less experienced than national officials[1] and their job is much harder – they have to deal with legal systems and local conditions that they know little about. They also have to adopt solutions that would work well across an array of different countries. No wonder many believe that international courts cause more harm than good.[2]

This chapter doesn't say anything about the professional abilities of international judges. Nevertheless, it argues that their intervention is often essential and can lead to good results, which states cannot reach on their own. International courts are uniquely positioned to learn from the collective wisdom of national decisions. The use of doctrines such as emerging consensus by the ECHR allows international courts to aggregate the independent decisions of numerous countries and make good policy decisions.

If states would try to learn from each other's experience, they would not decide independently and would end up following states that didn't make an independent decision themselves. In contrast, if international courts are allowed to intervene, states can make policy independently from each other. Later on, the international court will follow the majority

[1] *See* David Kosař, *Selecting Strasburg Judges, in* SELECTING EUROPE'S JUDGES: A CRITICAL REVIEW OF THE APPOINTMENT PROCEDURES TO THE EUROPEAN COURTS (Michal Bobek, ed., 2015) (arguing that the professional abilities of some ECHR judges are so low that they endanger the court's legitimacy)

[2] *See e.g.* SUSANNE K. SCHMIDT, THE EUROPEAN COURT OF JUSTICE AND THE POLICY PROCESS: THE SHADOW OF CASE LAW 235, 246–247 (2018) (arguing that by deciding cases based on distinct specific circumstances, the European Court of Justice leads to legal incoherence and uncertainty, generating bad policy outcomes).

of the states and set a policy that is likely to be better than any state can make on its own. States can then follow the international court's judgment and conform to this beneficial policy.

The interests of states may get in the way of this advantageous outcome. States may fail to decide independently for several different reasons. International courts can use certain doctrinal mechanisms, such as the margin of appreciation, to minimize this danger. Another problem has to do with the incentives of international judges themselves. Here, again, doctrinal solutions may prove helpful. Some of these mechanisms are discussed in this chapter.

A Why Use Comparative Law?

Many national courts refer to comparative law in their judgments. This practice seems like a reasonable way to learn from the experience of other states. If many foreign nations adopt a certain policy, this policy probably serves their interests well. Most nations try to adopt laws that they view as efficient and useful, or simply morally superior. A national court that is struggling to adopt laws with these qualities would do well to follow in the footsteps of other nations.

This basic intuition underlines a paper by Eric Posner and Cass Sunstein that advocates the use of comparative law.[3] The authors try to build on the intuition in an effort to maximize the benefits that could be gained by learning from the laws of other states. They do so by using a simple mathematical model that was developed by the eighteenth-century French philosopher Nicolas de Condorcet. The model is called the "Jury Theorem." It argues that when a group of decision-makers has to choose between two options – one right and one wrong – and each of the decision-makers has an equal probability greater than 50 percent of making the right choice, the majority's decision is more likely to be correct than that of any decision-maker. Furthermore, the larger the group, the higher the probability that the majority's decision will be correct.[4] Assuming that states choose their laws rationally, the Jury

[3] Posner & Sunstein, Note 1, Chapter 1.

[4] *Id* at 136, 141. To take a simple numerical example, consider a group that decides by majority vote in which every decision-maker has a 60 percent probablity to be right. If the group includes five decision-makers, it will have a 68.3 percent probablity of being right. For eleven decision-makers, this figure will be 75.3 percent. For twenty-one it will be 82.6 percent, and for fifty-one it will be 92.6 percent. If every member of the group has a 70 percent probablity of being right, the success rate of the group rises much more quickly.

Theorem would suggest following the laws adopted by the majority of the states in the world or in a certain region.

But the Jury Theorem works only under certain conditions. Posner and Sunstein identify three. First, the states examined adopted a policy based on a rational decision whose reasoning isn't fully revealed. If the decision wasn't based on some rational process, there is no reason to follow it. In contrast, if it is possible to track the actual reasons that led to the decision – for example, if the court is certain that a state annulled the death penalty only because it was proven not to deter crime – then the court could make an independent assessment of the death penalty based on the new scholarship about its inability to deter. When all the arguments used by others can be reviewed on the merits, there is no need to follow their decision. This is rarely the case, however. States usually make policy because of a mix of numerous arguments that either cannot be revealed or cannot be systematically weighed and balanced against each other.

The second condition is that states must be sufficiently similar to one another in order to justify learning from the laws of other states. If states are fundamentally different, the laws that are beneficial for some may actually prove harmful for others.

The third condition for the applicability of the Jury Theorem is that states make their decisions independently. This doesn't mean that states cannot rely on research or on arguments that were discovered by other states or draw inspiration from their experience. It does mean, however, that states which follow the policies of other states without making their own assessment of what constitutes the best policy violate the very reason for relying on the Jury Theorem.[5] That is where Posner and Sunstein's argument breaks down.

According to Posner and Sunstein, if national courts follow the laws of the majority of states in the world, they can make better policies than if they decide alone. All national courts profit from doing the same: They should shape the laws of their states based on what the majority of other states are doing. But if all states are changing the laws by following other states, as Posner and Sunstein recommend, then all states do not make

Five members will render a probability of 83.7 percent, eleven members will render 92.2 percent, twenty-one members will render 97.4 percent, and with fifty-one members the right choice is almost inevitable – 99.9 percent probablity that the majority will decide correctly.

5 *Id*, at 144–145.

policy independently. When policy isn't made independently, there is no justification to follow the laws of most states. In fact, if states do not decide independently but instead follow each other, they may form what Posner and Sunstein call "information cascades": states will follow states that mimicked other states and didn't make policy independently.[6]

Posner and Sunstein are well aware of this problem. They realize that they cannot offer the same recommendation to all states. Every state that learns from others may improve its own decision, but it corrupts the pool of information that can serve other states if they wish to do the same.

Theoretically, one can imagine a world in which some states make policy independently and other states aggregate the decision of this group and follow the majority's decision. It is unclear, however, how states can tell each other apart. How can they know which states consistently decide independently and which states simply follow other states? If the group of states that decide independently are fundamentally different than all other states, they may be recognized. But such differences may also imply that the laws that suit the two groups of states should not be the same. The second condition for the applicability of the Jury Theorem specifies that only similar states should learn from each other.

Another possibility is that national courts do not blindly follow the laws of other states.[7] Instead, they assess the arguments that were used in other states on the merits and examine their laws with a critical eye. This would prevent an information cascade from materializing since every court makes some form of independent judgment before setting policy. That seems like a very realistic picture of the world. A lot of courts that use comparative law do exactly that: they draw inspiration from other systems or they examine the validity of arguments used in other states. This decision-making process may be very useful, but it doesn't profit from the advantage of the Jury Theorem. The first condition for the applicability of the Jury Theorem is that it aggregates the decision-making capacity of rational others. This implies following the decision of others, not analyzing the reasons behind their decision. Those reasons are usually hidden or incommensurable anyway, which is exactly why the Jury Theorem is needed.

The theory apart, many courts probably do make independent judgments. Besides, the laws of states are also determined by the parliament and the executive, which often make policy independently. This implies

[6] *Id*, at 163.
[7] *Id*.

that learning from the laws of other states isn't a completely futile exercise, even if every state that follows this advice ruins it for all the others.

International courts can improve on this imperfect situation.

B Why International Courts Are Better than National Courts

If all the states in a region make their policies independently, the Jury Theorem implies that the law adopted by the majority of the states is probably good. If an international court follows the majority of the states and issues a judgment that is complied with by all the states in the region, then all states gain the full benefit of comparative law.

The unique advantage of international courts is simply institutional. National courts can either follow each other and form a cascade or decide independently and gain no benefit from comparative law. An international court that uses comparative law allows all the states to make an initial independent decision and provides them, at a later stage, with a decision that perfectly aggregates the policies of all states.

1 *The Emerging Consensus Doctrine*

There are several doctrines in international law that direct international courts to learn from the decisions of states. The doctrine that best fits the analysis here is the emerging consensus doctrine used by the ECHR. Recent empirical research suggests that the ECHR uses this doctrine to interpret the European Convention on Human Rights as safeguarding any right that is protected by the majority of the states in Europe. In a sense, the ECHR follows the majority of the states in Europe and requires all states in the region to live up to the standards of human rights set by the majority of the states.[8]

An interview with a former judge of the ECHR explains how emerging consensus is actually discovered by the judges. When the ECHR sits in Grand Chamber cases, which are legally important cases referred to a panel of seventeen judges, the research division of the court would often write a comparative analysis of the laws in all – or at least most of – the

[8] *See* Helfer & Voeten, Note 2, Chapter 1 at 106. *See also* Kanstantsin Dzehtsiarou, European Consensus and the Legitimacy of the European Court of Human Rights 12, 37 (2015) (arguing that the ECHR usually identifies an emerging consensus when there is a significant majority of states protecting a certain right, even if not all states do that).

states in Europe. This analysis will sometimes include a short description of the law in each European state, but it is sometimes limited to answering a specific identical question about the state of the law in each state. If a substantial majority of states adopt a certain legal solution, or if more than half of the states adopt that solution and it is also supported by a growing trend across Europe, judges can use emerging consensus as an argument to adopt this solution as the binding interpretation of the Convention. The comparative analysis is sometimes only a minor supportive tool, but it would sometimes affect the result and then judges will usually specifically mention the emerging consensus doctrine in their judgment. While judges do not always follow the emerging consensus, they are sometimes criticized for digressing from it by dissenting judges. Judges may be convinced not to follow emerging consensus because states should be given a margin of appreciation or because of respect for profound moral values of the states.[9]

Empirical research also suggests that states do not follow what seems to be the majority in Europe themselves. Instead, they change their policies to conform to the judgments of the ECHR only after they are issued, even if they are issued against another state.[10] This suggests that states are deciding independently. The ECHR is provided with numerous independent choices of the states which it uses to find the optimal policy under the Jury Theorem logic. This policy is set in the court's judgments. Because states comply with these judgments, they internalize the full benefit that can be gained from comparative law.

2 *Potential Criticism*

Section 3.C is dedicated to investigating situations in which the use of emerging consensus should be limited or modified, for example by applying the margin of appreciation doctrine. But before addressing these challenges, one must consider some more fundamental criticisms against applying the Jury Theorem logic to emerging consensus. Following the majority's decision in a group will only lead to good policies if every member of the group is more than 50 percent likely to be correct. If members are more likely to be wrong than to be right, increasing the

[9] Interview with David Thór Björgvinsson, a former judge of the ECHR, Sept. 13, 2016.
[10] *See* Helfer & Voeten, Note 2, Chapter 1 at 106.

number of decision-makers would only make the collective decision worse.

What if states are more likely to make laws that oppress their citizens than laws that protect them? In that case, a European consensus that favors restrictions on human rights is certainly possible.[11] If most states are ruled by political majorities and abuse the rights of minorities, then minorities will be discriminated across all of Europe and the emerging consensus doctrine may not be able to rescue them.[12] If all states are showing an unwarranted resistance to refugees, for example, following the majority of states would not lead to a better result.

There are several answers to this criticism. Starting with the actual conditions in Europe today, scholars have brought evidence that the fears of an abusive use of emerging consensus are largely unmerited. Usually, emerging consensus is used to protect minorities – the ECHR used emerging consensus several times to require higher standards of minorities' protection. In fact, when the majority of states in Europe violate the rights of minorities, the court will often resort to its judicial discretion and decide not to apply emerging consensus. Moreover, it is important to stress that standards of human rights protection in Europe are generally quite high, justifying the use of emerging consensus to follow what most European states deem to be good policy.[13]

These answers are, of course, contingent on specific facts that can change and can also be contested. But there is also a general and theoretical response to the criticism. Even if every state has certain minorities and every state discriminates against them in certain ways, there is no reason to believe that all states have exactly the same minorities and discriminate against them in exactly the same ways. If states do not discriminate in exactly the same manner, they would not push an abusive European consensus in the same direction. To take a simple example: If a third of the states violate the freedom of speech, another third violate the right of privacy, and another third violate the right to a fair trial, emerging consensus would require states to protect

[11] *See* Jeffrey A. Brauch, *The Margin of Appreciation and the Jurisprudence of the European Court of Human Rights: Threat to the Rule of Law*, 11 Colum. J. Eur. L. 113, 146–147 (2005); Paolo G. Carozza, *Uses and Misuses of Comparative Law in International Human Rights: Some Reflections on the Jurisprudence of the European Court of Human Rights*, 73 Notre Dame L. Rev. 1217, 1231 (1998).

[12] *See* Benvenisti, Note 79, Chapter 2 at 851.

[13] *See* Dzehtsiarou, Note 8 at 122–129 (making these factual arguments and providing numerous examples to support them).

every one of these three rights. The Jury Theorem itself is based on conceding that every decision-maker is biased, but because decision-makers are not biased in the same direction, their biases will balance themselves out and the majority of the group will make a better decision than each individual member.[14]

Finally, before dismissing the use of emerging consensus, one must consider the alternative. Is deferring to the state a better alternative than requiring it to conform to the European consensus? Chapter 2 argues that when minority rights are at stake judicial intervention is legitimate because the state cannot be trusted to protect its minorities. Maybe Europe as a whole cannot be trusted as well, but it is certainly not less trustable than one European state. Alternatively, the ECHR may decide to rely on moral principles to justify intervention in the practice of the states. Clearly, sometimes this should be done. But moral principles are contested and controversial. Their application would often seem arbitrary and damage the legitimacy of the court.[15] Emerging consensus isn't a foolproof method, but all the alternatives may be worse.

There is yet another theoretical challenge to the use of emerging consensus to improve human rights protection across Europe. The ECHR uses emerging consensus to set a minimum, a "floor," of human rights protection that is required from all states. States are free to grant *more* protection than this floor. They are only constrained not to grant *less* protection. But this picture is a bit too simplistic. Human rights are often relational and when the ECHR requires protection of one right, it may inevitably limit the protection of another right – setting a "ceiling" for its protection. When the court protects the freedom of speech of some, it limits the rights of others to protect their privacy.[16]

This challenge may pose some rhetorical problems for the ECHR, but it doesn't pose a problem for the application of the Jury Theorem logic. In fact, it confirms the usefulness of the Jury Theorem as a decisional tool for resolving difficult dilemmas. If a right has been violated by a specific state – even if other rights and interests are protected as a result – the

[14] *See* Maxwell L. Stearns, *The Condorcet Jury Theorem and Judicial Decisionmaking: A Reply to Saul Levmore*, 3 Theo. Inq. L. 125, 130–131 (2002).

[15] *See* Dzehtsiarou, Note 8 at 117–118.

[16] *See* Federico Fabbrini, Fundamental Rights in Europe: Challenges and Transformations in a Comparative Perspective 38–39 (2014).

ECHR can apply emerging consensus to check if the majority of states in Europe allow the violation of this right. If the majority of states do not allow the violation of this right, either because they do not consider the concomitant protection of other rights a sufficient excuse for the violation or for any other reason, then there is reason to believe that the violation is unjustified. In such cases, the ECHR can use the emerging consensus doctrine to find the state in violation of the Convention.

3 *Other Doctrines Used by International Courts*

The emerging consensus doctrine seems to fit perfectly the logic behind the Jury Theorem. This is why it will be the focus of the chapter. But there are other doctrines used by international courts that reflect to some extent the decisional benefit of the Jury Theorem. Take multilateral treaties, for example. They are based on the agreement of several states that together undertake to conform to a certain legal standard. Treaties that are almost universal represent a view that is shared across numerous states and probably reflect good policies. The problem with treaties, though, is that they do not stem from independent choices of states. States join treaties based on a negotiation with other states in which they give up some of their interests in return for concessions from other countries. Some states even join treaties because they are pressured to do so by other countries or offered some sort of payment for their willingness to join.[17] States can also join treaties and then fail to comply with them, which indicates they do not view their international commitments as reflecting their independent interest. Because joining a treaty does not always constitute an independent policy choice, counting states that ratify treaties would not necessarily lead to the optimal rule under the Jury Theorem logic.

The sources of international law, as specified in article 38 of the Statute of the ICJ, include in addition to treaties also international custom and "general principles of law recognized by civilized nations." International custom reflects a policy that states accepted as a general practice, out of a sense of legal duty. If many states behave in a certain way and form a custom, this custom may reflect the independent policy choices of numerous states. It enjoys the decisional benefit of the Jury Theorem. The same applies to legal principles that were adopted across most of the

[17] Posner & Sunstein, Note 1, Chapter 1 at 165–166.

states. This source of international law refers the court to independent legal choices of most of the world's countries and consequently enjoys a decisional advantage. Another subsidiary source of international law mentioned in article 38 is the judgments of other courts. To the extent that international law tends to follow what most national courts are doing, it will also enjoy the advantage of the Jury Theorem.

In recent years, scholars have noted that states adopt different interpretations of international law, a phenomenon that was named "comparative international law."[18] If international courts tend to follow the interpretations of international law that are common to most states, they will make a decision that concurs with the logic of the Jury Theorem.

The sources mentioned in article 38 are shaping the judgments of the ICJ. This court, therefore, reflects in its decisions the logic of the Jury Theorem, at least partly. Intervention by the ICJ can consequently help states make better laws. Furthermore, article 38 is recognized as stating the general sources of international law. Other international courts that follow these sources in their judgments also enjoy this decisional advantage and can support their intervention in domestic affairs based on the claim that they can help states make better law.

Even if an international criminal court, to take a remote example, uses these international law doctrines to guide its judgments in criminal matters, it can justify its decisions by reference to the Jury Theorem. The International Criminal Tribunal for the Former Yugoslavia (ICTY) in the famous *Erdemovic* case discovered general principles of law that limit the applicability of the criminal defense of duress. The ICTY discovered these principles by relying on judgments and laws from numerous states, in a way that concurs with the Jury Theorem logic.[19]

While states that use international law can access the same sources, their institutional position will quickly lead to a cascade that will make state decisions dependent on each other and pull the rug under the Jury Theorem logic. The advantage of international courts doesn't stem from the quality of international judges or even from the legal sources they use. It stems from the institutional position of international courts that allows them to aggregate the decisions of states without violating the rule that states must decide independently.

[18] *See* Comparative International Law (Anthea Roberts et al., eds., Oxford University Press, 2018).

[19] Prosecutor v. Erdemovic, IT-96-22-T ICTY Trial Chamber I (1996) at par. 19.

C Problems Undermining the Advantage of Emerging Consensus

The emerging consensus doctrine is an ideal example for illustrating the advantage international courts have in applying the Jury Theorem to reach better decisions. Nevertheless, even when the ECHR applies emerging consensus, certain problems may occur that conflict with the conditions under which the Jury Theorem works best. This chapter reviews these problems. It also suggests doctrinal solutions that may help restore the decisional advantage of the ECHR despite them.

1 Some States Are Different

As explained at the start of this section, learning from the experience of other states is only justified if states are similar to one another. Different states may thrive under different legal solutions. The ECHR is likely to gain more from comparative law than a court with worldwide jurisdiction because the ECHR deals only with democracies that share the same region and the same history. But even in Europe some states are different than others. Some of these differences are relevant to the issues discussed by the ECHR and should affect its decision.

A powerful example is the *Sahin case.*[20] This case dealt with a female Muslim student who viewed the wearing of an Islamic headscarf as her religious duty. The applicant argued that the regulations in her Turkish university that prevented her from wearing the headscarf violate her right to freedom of religion protected by the Convention. She proved that the only country in Europe that forbids the wearing of an Islamic headscarf at universities is Turkey. Turkey's position doesn't just contradict the majority of states in Europe; it contradicts the policies of all the other states, without exception.

Despite the clear consensus against the Turkish law, the court decided not to find a violation. It stressed that Turkey is different from the other European States. Turkey has a predominantly Muslim population. The country's history and fear of Islamic extremism strongly committed it to secularism.[21] In short, laws that suit the rest of Europe do not suit Turkey, because Turkey is not similar enough to the rest of Europe across relevant parameters.

[20] Case of Leyla Sahin v. Turkey, judgment of November 10, 2005.

[21] *Id* at par. 114–123. For criticism on this decision see the dissenting opinion of judge Tulkens at par. 3.

The ECHR's decision not to find Turkey in violation is based on the margin of appreciation doctrine. This doctrine is often presented as competing with the emerging consensus doctrine. Generally speaking, the clearer the consensus in Europe, the less likely it is that the ECHR will defer to state policies that go against the consensus and cover these policies by the margin of appreciation.[22] Yet viewing emerging consensus and margin of appreciation as competing is too simplistic. The *Sahin* case demonstrates that some state policies call for a margin of appreciation even if most states are committed to an opposite policy – for example, because the state in question is different from the rest of Europe. The next subsections will demonstrate that the margin of appreciation can also be used to give states an incentive to make independent decisions, a vital condition for allowing the emerging consensus doctrine to render optimal results.

2 The Court Could Manipulate Its Decisions

The ECHR is tasked with interpreting the Convention, a task that involves a significant amount of discretion. As the court uses its discretion to apply the law, it has to face a series of political constraints. If states in Europe are dissatisfied with the court's judgments, they can seriously hurt the court. States can fail to comply with judgments of the ECHR, they can criticize the court, attempt to change the Convention, or leave the Convention regime altogether.[23] All these forms of backlash should be considered by the court as it makes its decisions. The court cannot go on suicide missions. It cannot uphold an emerging consensus when doing so would jeopardize the court's future.

This reality puts the ECHR in a cruel dilemma. When faced with the possibility of backlash, it could enforce the emerging consensus sincerely and bear the harmful consequences, or it could misapply the emerging consensus to find the state in compliance with the Convention. The problem with misapplying emerging consensus is that the court would be giving false guidance to all the states in Europe. Emerging consensus is

[22] Case of Evans v. The United Kingdom, judgment of April 10, 2007, at par. 77; Laurence R. Helfer & Anne-Marie Slaughter, *Toward a Theory of Effective Supranational Adjudication*, 107 Yale L.J. 273, 316–317 (1997); Benvenisti, Note 79, Chapter 2 at 851.

[23] Laurence R. Helfer & Anne-Marie Slaughter, *Why States Create International Tribunals: A Response to Professors Posner and Yoo*, 93 Cal. L. Rev. 899, 942–944 (2005); Ginsburg, Note 3, Chapter 1 at 632; Dothan, Note 3, Chapter 1.

useful because it can aggregate the decisions of all European states and set this solution as a rule for all Europe. When that rule is distorted for political reasons, all Europe is led in the wrong direction.

The ECHR can use the margin of appreciation doctrine to solve this dilemma. The doctrine allows the ECHR not to find the state in violation without indicating that its actions concur with the emerging consensus in Europe. In fact, the ECHR can indicate within the judgment that the state's practices contradict the emerging consensus. It can supply the contours of the emerging consensus for the benefit of all states in Europe that become aware of this judgment. At the same time, the court would defer to the policy of the state in the case at hand and avoid a finding of violation. Without finding a violation, the state is denied the ability not to comply with the court. The incentive of the state to use other mechanisms of backlash to hurt the court is also substantially curtailed. Using the margin of appreciation is a compromise because it shields the imperfect policies of the respondent state. Yet it can supply Europe with the correct guidance without causing a reprisal against the court.

The ECHR traditionally used the margin of appreciation to avoid misinterpreting the Convention without raising the wrath of powerful states. A good example is the case of *Ireland* v. *The United Kingdom*.[24] In this judgment, the court found that some interrogation techniques used by the United Kingdom to combat terrorism in Ireland in the 1970s violated the Convention. However, the vital measure of administrative detentions was granted the margin of appreciation and wasn't branded as violating the Convention. The ECHR stressed that the United Kingdom is better suited to decide what emergency measures are needed.[25] By using the margin of appreciation, the court avoided a direct confrontation with the United Kingdom, but didn't grant a stamp of approval for its actions either.

3 *The Court Could Delay Its Decisions*

When the ECHR faces unacceptable backlash, it has another option besides manipulating its judgment. The court could effectively decide not to decide. While the ECHR has to decide all the cases that reach it –

[24] Case of Ireland v. The United Kingdom, judgment of January 18, 1978, at par. 207, 214.
[25] *Id*, at par. 207, 214.

besides cases that clearly do not involve a significant human rights infringement[26] – it can avoid delicate cases by determining that they are out of its jurisdiction. If the ECHR uses its ability to determine its own jurisdiction strategically, it can dodge delicate cases for years, until political conditions change and the court thinks it is able to issue an appropriate judgment.

An example for such a strategy is the *Bankovic* case.[27] In this case, citizens of the Federal Republic of Yugoslavia initiated an application against seventeen European states that are members of NATO. The application argued that by participating in a NATO airstrike in Yugoslavia that killed civilians, these states violated the right to life protected by the Convention. The ECHR decided that it doesn't have jurisdiction to hear the case because the airstrike happened outside of the territory of all European members of the Convention.

Many criticized the *Bankovic* case as digressing from earlier judgments of the ECHR that found European states responsible for extraterritorial violations.[28] However, by not exercising its jurisdiction, the ECHR avoided a clash with many of the most powerful countries in Europe. The *Bankovic case* created an ambiguity in the ECHR's doctrine regarding extra-territorial violations. This ambiguity wasn't resolved until ten years later when the *Al-Skeini*[29] and *Al-Jedda*[30] judgments found the United Kingdom responsible for violations in occupied Iraq. It was only these cases that clearly stipulated that member states that

[26] Under article 35(3) to the Convention the ECHR shall declare that an application is inadmissible if it is "manifestly ill-founded, or an abuse of the right of individual application," or if the applicant has not suffered a "significant disadvantage" unless respect for human rights requires deciding the case and provided that the case has been considered by a domestic tribunal.

[27] Bankovic and others v. Belgium and Others, Decision of December 12, 2001, EUR. Ct. H.R. 2001-XII 333.

[28] For criticism of the judgment *see*: Ruth & Trilsch, Note 48, Chapter 2 at 172; Alexander Orakhelashvili, *Restrictive Interpretation of Human Rights Treaties in the Recent Jurisprudence of the European Court of Human Rights*, 14 EUR. J. INT'L L. 529, 545 (2003). For previous judgments creating responsibility for extra-territorial actions *see*: Case of Loizidou v. Turkey (Preliminary Objections) Judgment of March 23, 1995, EUR. Ct. H.R. (ser. A) 310 at pp. 23–24 par. 62, Case of Loizidou v. Turkey, judgment of December 18, 1996 (merits) *Reports of Judgments and Decisions* 1996-VI at pages 2234–2235 par. 52. Cyprus v. Turkey, Judgment of May 10, 2001, *Reports of Judgments and Decisions,* 2001-IV, par. 78. *See* the analysis in Note 48, Chapter 2

[29] Case of Al-Skeini and others v. The United Kingdom, judgment of July 7, 2011.

[30] Case of Al-Jedda v. The United Kingdom, judgment of July 7, 2011.

commit violations in the territory of states that were never members of the Convention can still be held liable before the ECHR.

The ECHR had to wait a decade before it could assert its extraterritorial jurisdiction. European states and the European public were ready to accept criticism of the war in Iraq in 2011, while criticism of the war in Yugoslavia in 2001 was probably unacceptable.[31] Similar political constraints may force the ECHR to avoid making a decision for years, as could delays caused by the sheer amount of cases waiting to be resolved. The states, however, may not be willing to wait that long.

If the ECHR takes years to make its decision, the result is that states are stuck with the legal policies they made independently instead of being guided by the court. Realizing that, the states may decide to use comparative law in the hope of making better policies immediately instead of waiting for the court to make its decision. When one state decides to use comparative law, there is no problem. But when many states start to learn from each other, their policies are no longer independently made. In fact, states will fall into the same information cascades that result from adopting the Posner and Sunstein recommendation for the use of comparative law by national courts. If the ECHR decided, years later, to use emerging consensus and learn from the majority of the states, it will face state policies that were not made independently and its decision will not enjoy the advantages of the Jury Theorem.

To give states an incentive to decide independently, the ECHR must issue its judgments relatively quickly. This way, states may be convinced to make their policies by themselves, since they know they would soon be given the opportunity to follow the ECHR's judgment that aggregates the collective wisdom of all the states in Europe.

The margin of appreciation doctrine allows the ECHR to avoid unnecessary delays. When faced with the possibility of dangerous political backlash, the ECHR could defer to the state's policies, while indicating the correct standard derived from the emerging consensus doctrine. Because the state isn't found in violation, the chances it will seriously harm the court are minimized. At the same time, all the other states can be motivated to make their policies independently and change them only to follow a standard that was clearly indicated by the ECHR, even if no violation was found in the case at hand.

[31] *See* Shai Dothan, *How International Courts Enhance Their Legitimacy*, 14 THEO. INQ. L. 455, 475–476 (2013).

If states rely on the ECHR to issue its judgments quickly, they are more likely to decide independently. At the same time, states that realize they can change their policies quickly to follow the optimal standard dictated by the ECHR may invest fewer resources in making good policy. The smaller the effort that states invest in making their policies, the less successful these policies would probably be. Ultimately, when the ECHR tries to aggregate state policies by using emerging consensus, it will be aggregating weaker policies. Fortunately, the majority decision in a group as large as that of the forty-seven states in Europe is likely to be correct even if every decision-maker is only slightly better than an arbitrary decision.[32] Even if European states invest little resources in making their policy, the policies adopted by the majority are quite likely to be good.

4 *States Could Act Strategically to Avoid Violation Findings*

If the ECHR finds a state in violation of the Convention, this finding can damage the state's reputation. A violation finding signals that the state doesn't care enough about its reputation to fulfill its international obligations. Other states may deduce from this signal that the violating state cannot be trusted and would offer it worse deals in international negotiations. Losing reputation has a clear financial cost.[33]

To avoid a loss of reputation, states may try to predict the judgments of the ECHR and conform to them in advance, before the court has occasion to find them in violation. If states know that the court uses emerging consensus, they may try to follow what the majority of states in Europe are doing in order to preempt a judgment that would impose on them the same standard and find them in violation.

But why stop there? If states know that all states in Europe are trying to avoid findings of violation, they would quickly realize that all states would try to guess what the majority of states are doing. A dynamic known in game theory as a *beauty contest* would arise.[34] All states would try to guess what the majority of states think the majority will

[32] For a simple numerical example, see Note 4.

[33] *See* Andrew T. Guzman, How International Law Works – A Rational Choice Theory 33–36 (2008).

[34] This unique situation in which all participants try to guess what the majority will decide was named "beauty contest" after a metaphor used by John Maynard Keynes. Keynes described a situation in which readers of a magazine have to choose the six prettiest pictures of models out of a list of one hundred. Those that choose the six that get the most votes win a prize, giving everyone an interest in guessing what the others will do instead

do, or what the majority thinks that the majority thinks the majority will do, and so on. States will try to identify trends in the behavior of other states in an attempt not to be stuck with policies held by the minority. The result is that states will not make policy independently and the majority of the states will not hold the decisional benefits of the Jury Theorem.

The root of the problem lies with the fact that states are afraid of a judgment against them but are not sure what will be the standard applied in this judgment. This is why they turn to guesses about the views of the majority of the states. The best way to prevent this fear is to provide the states with a proper warning – a declaration of the standard that will be imposed prior to a finding of violation. The margin of appreciation doctrine can help the court do exactly that. It allows the court to declare the standard that will be required across Europe, without finding the examined state in violation of the Convention.

An example that can illustrate this strategy is the series of judgments that the ECHR issued regarding the rights of transsexuals in the United Kingdom. In 1986, the ECHR issued the *Rees* case,[35] in which it used the margin of appreciation to defer to the policies of the United Kingdom regarding transsexuals. The court decided that maintaining the original sex of transsexuals in their birth certificate – which they have to present on some occasions – as well as preventing them from marrying a person of their opposite current sex do not constitute a violation of the Convention. At the same time, the court and the commission, then serving as the first tier of review, pointed out that several European countries protect transsexuals even though there is no clear consensus on the matter.[36] The court also stressed that it is aware of the suffering of transsexuals and noted that the issue should be reviewed in light of scientific and social developments.

In its later judgments, the ECHR repeatedly warned the United Kingdom that its policies are problematic. In the *Cossey* case,[37] the court highlighted the severity of the problem and the need to review the issue. In the *Sheffield and Horsham* case,[38] the court expressed clear discontent

of making a sincere choice. *See* JOHN MAYNARD KEYNES, THE GENERAL THEORY OF EMPLOYMENT, INTEREST AND MONEY (Atlantic 2008) at 140.

35 Rees v. The United Kingdom, judgment of October 17, 1986 EUR. Ct. H.R. (ser. A) 106.

36 *See id* at par. 37; the Commission's Report of December 12, 1984 at par. 44.

37 *Cossey* case, judgment of September 27, 1990 EUR. Ct. H.R. (ser. A) 184, at 17.

38 Sheffield and Horsham v. The United Kingdom, judgment of July 30, 1998, 1998-V EUR. Ct. H.R. 2011, 2029.

with the United Kingdom's policy. Moreover, the court stated that only four out of thirty-seven states that were reviewed in Europe prevent transsexuals from changing their sex in their birth certificate. This statement clarifies that the emerging consensus in Europe contradicts the policies of the United Kingdom.

After warning the United Kingdom repeatedly for more than fifteen years, the ECHR eventually found it in violation of the Convention in the *Goodwin* case,[39] which was issued in 2002. The ECHR indicated that the majority of states in Europe are opposed to the United Kingdom's policies years before *Goodwin*. In fact, *Sheffield and Horsham* counted the states in Europe and made the consensus abundantly clear. Initially, the ECHR protected the United Kingdom from a finding of violation in order to give it a proper warning. Only after the court made it clear that the United Kingdom was transgressing the Convention and gave it ample opportunity to change its practices and after the court's repeated warnings were left unheeded, did the court issue a violation finding.

The message that may have been intended by this practice should be received not only by the United Kingdom, but by all European states. The ECHR strives to make states realize that they will not be found in violation if they listen to the court's warning and change their practices within a reasonable time. This allows states to make independent decisions without having to guess the majority that is forming in Europe. Only after the ECHR aggregates the independent decisions of states and presents the emerging consensus as a warning for the rest of Europe should states change their practices to conform to that policy.

5 *States Do Not Decide Simultaneously*

The Jury Theorem relies on aggregating rational decisions by multiple decision-makers. If every decision-maker is more likely to be right than wrong, the group is more likely to be correct than every individual decision-maker. When states make their policies after a public and parliamentary debate, or when national courts set policy in their judgments, it seems natural to regard these policies as the result of a rational decision. But what if relevant conditions have recently changed and the state is still deliberating on how to change its policies? If the state doesn't

[39] Christine Goodwin v. The United Kingdom, judgment of July 11, 2002, 2002-VI EUR. Ct. H.R. 1.

forbid a behavior that becomes hazardous due to changing conditions, it still has a policy on the issue: The behavior in question isn't forbidden. Yet this policy isn't a result of deliberation. It is only a default position that may prove inadequate in light of current conditions. The ECHR should not aggregate default positions in states that did not exhaust the deliberation on the topic together with policies that were changed as a result of a real decision-making process.

The judgment in the *S.A.S* case[40] reflects this understanding. The case concerned a French law that forbade Muslim women from wearing a full-face veil. At the time, France and Belgium were the only two states in Europe that prohibited concealing the face in public.[41] It may seem as if a clear majority in Europe contradicts the French policy, forming an emerging consensus. Yet the ECHR decided that other states in Europe are still considering their law and did not reach a final decision on the matter. Furthermore, in many states in Europe there are so few women that wear a full-face veil that the conditions for making policy on this issue have not yet materialized in these countries.

In essence, the ECHR decided that the policy in most European states on the issue of Muslim full-face veils is not a rational decision. It is only a default position – because the veil isn't specifically prohibited, it is allowed. Consequently, there is no real emerging consensus on this issue.[42]

The result of the *S.A.S* case can certainly be criticized. For example, judges Nussberger and Jäderblom argued in their dissenting opinion in this case that states in Europe didn't avoid the decision on the prohibition of full-face veils. Rather, they decided against making any legislation on the topic.[43] The facts of such a complex case can be read in multiple ways, but the principle that guided the majority opinion remains valid. When conditions in Europe significantly changed and some states didn't adjust their laws to deal with the new situation, their current policies are default positions and not the result of a rational decision-making process. Such policies cannot be aggregated to form an emerging consensus that enjoys the decisional benefit of the Jury Theorem.

[40] S.A.S v. France, judgment of July 1, 2014.
[41] *Id* at par. 40.
[42] *Id* at par. 156.
[43] *Id*, at par. 19 of their dissenting opinion.

6 *Decisions Involving Several Options*

The Jury Theorem is a way to aggregate the decisions of many decision-makers even if their motives are unknown or incommensurable. As long as the decision-makers have to choose between only two options, following the majority's decision may draw from the collective wisdom of the group and point to the better course of action even if every decision-maker has a different set of reasons. When there are more than two options, however, the Jury Theorem sometimes cannot help to choose the best option.

This exception to the Jury Theorem, which is known as the Condorcet Paradox, shows that when decision-makers have to choose between more than two options, their choice may not be transitive. This means that the group would end up preferring A over B or B over A depending on the way the votes of the decision-makers are counted.

In many factual situations, there are more than two available courses of action and the Condorcet Paradox is a real possibility. This possibility could materialize if the decision-makers are basing their decision on several conflicting considerations. States that choose one out of several possible policies based on different reasons may form a situation in which the Jury Theorem doesn't apply and there is no justification to apply emerging consensus.

The ECHR has shown some awareness of this problem and has been reluctant to recognize emerging consensus when states make their choices based on different considerations. The argument between the judges in the *A, B, and C* case[44] may illustrate this point. The case concerned the right of women to have an abortion in Ireland. The majority opinion ruled that although most countries in Europe allow abortion there is no consensus on the issue because there is no consensus whether a fetus is a living human being. The majority therefore decided that there is no emerging consensus contradicting Ireland's policy of limiting abortions.[45] In contrast, a dissenting opinion of six judges argued that the European stance on whether fetuses are alive is irrelevant. The question before the court, they argued, is only whether in the final balancing of the right of the fetus and of the mother there is a policy for or against abortion. The European consensus on that is clear: it prefers the rights of the mother

[44] Case of A, B, and C v. Ireland, judgment of December 16, 2010.

[45] *Id*, at par. 237.

over those of the fetus.[46] A concurring opinion of judge Geoghegan adopts an even stricter test than that of the majority for applying emerging consensus. Judge Geoghegan argued that the question is whether the states in Europe properly took into account and balanced all the competing considerations on the issue. Because in some European countries there is no similar public interest in protecting the right of the unborn child as there is in Ireland, the states are not undertaking the same balancing and no real emerging consensus can be identified.[47]

The ECHR judges in *A, B, and C* realize that complex legal policies are more than a choice between two options. They also realize that this implies the reasons behind the choice of policy may be important and cannot be ignored. Before the policies of states could be aggregated, the judges must decide if states are actually making policy in light of similar considerations. The majority opinion and judge Geoghegan stressed that because the states made their policies based on different world views, the policy of the so-called majority is meaningless.

To demonstrate how choosing between several options based on contrasting world views could lead to the Condorcet Paradox, consider another issue the ECHR has dealt with – the right of prisoners to vote. In the *Hirst* case,[48] the ECHR discussed whether a blanket ban on the right of prisoners to vote in the United Kingdom violates the Convention. The court reviewed the laws in Europe and found eighteen European states that allow prisoners to vote without any constraint, thirteen European states (including the United Kingdom) that prevent all prisoners from voting, and twelve European states that deny the right to vote from some prisoners under certain conditions.[49] The conditions set by the countries that prevent only some of the prisoners from voting include the number of prison years in the verdict, the severity of the crime, and the connection between the crime and the democratic process. Some countries give the convicting judge discretion whether to deny the convict the right to vote.[50]

[46] *Id*, at par. 2 to the joint partly dissenting opinion of judges Rozakis, Tulkens, Fura, Hirvelä, Malinverni, and Poalelungi.

[47] *Id*, at par. 9 to Geoghegan's opinion.

[48] Hirst v. The United Kingdom (No. 2), judgment of October 6, 2005, 2005-IX EUR. Ct. H.R. 187.

[49] *Id*, at par. 33.

[50] For a summary of the laws on this issue in European states *see* Shai Dothan, *Comparative Views on the Right to Vote in International Law: The Case of Prisoners' Disenfranchisement, in* COMPARATIVE INTERNATIONAL LAW 379, 382–386 (Anthea Roberts et al., eds., 2018).

The states in Europe therefore choose between at least three options: (A) allow all prisoners to vote; (B) deny the right to vote from some of the prisoners under certain conditions; (C) deny the right to vote from all prisoners. The policy chosen by the state doesn't indicate the underlying considerations behind their policy but analyzing the judgments of states from around the world suggests that there are at least three potential views on the topic: (1) the right to vote is an inalienable right; it cannot be taken away; (2) voting is a revocable right; it belongs to the voters but may be taken away under some conditions; (3) voting is a privilege that doesn't belong to citizens; they may only use it under certain conditions.[51] Even in the simple case of three countries holding these contrasting views and choosing between the three policies that divide European countries on the issue, situations of intransitivity may occur in which the Jury Theorem cannot hold.

Countries that view voting as an inalienable right will certainly prefer policy A over all others. Their choice between policies B and C isn't certain, but it is at least possible that they would prefer B over C in order to let as many prisoners as possible vote.

Countries that view voting as a revocable right would clearly favor policy B. It isn't clear what would be their second-best policy. Some of these countries may view disenfranchisement as largely symbolic and would never support the disenfranchisement of all prisoners. However, it is possible that some of these countries are completely averse to letting some criminals vote, for example those that committed severe crimes. When given a choice, these countries would prefer policy C over policy A and deny the right to vote to all prisoners rather than give the vote to the group of prisoners they detest.

Countries that view voting as a privilege would ideally choose policy C since they believe that prisoners violated the social contract and do not deserve to vote.[52] Their second-best and third-best policies are contestable. Some of these countries view the stigma associated with "civic death" that results from disenfranchisement as paramount. After all, in most countries the disenfranchisement of prisoners couldn't affect election results and is more a question of principle than of actual consequence.[53]

[51] *See id* at 386–390.

[52] Susan Easton, *The Prisoner's Right to Vote and Civic Responsibility: Reaffirming the Social Contract?* 56 Probation J. 224, 227–228 (2009).

[53] The United States may be an exception – a unique case where prisoners' disenfranchisement may actually change elections results. This is due to the high number of prisoners, the strict disenfranchisement policies that in some states extend after incarceration is over, and the large number of black prisoners who are usually considered as democratic

Some countries may therefore prefer policy A over policy B and let all prisoners vote in order not to discriminate between prisoners in a way that would contradict the message they want to send by disenfranchisement. When the decision is one of principle, it is possible that the equal treatment of prisoners would rank higher than the number of prisoners that would really be disenfranchised.

Table 3.1 presents the hypothetical preferences listed in this section:

Table 3.1 *The hypothetical preferences of states with different views on voting rights*

	First best	Second best	Third best
(1) Voting as an inalienable right	A	B	C
(2) Voting as a revocable right	B	C	A
(3) Voting as a privilege	C	A	B

Apparently, most countries (two out of three) prefer A over B. Most countries prefer B over C. But most countries also prefer C over A. If the preferences of most countries rank as A>B>C>A, the preferences of the countries are not transitive.

The lack of transitivity stems from the fact that states calculate several considerations when they set the order of their preferences. For example, states care both about the question whether prisoners will vote and about treating prisoners equally. Legal systems deal with complex cases like that all the time. But usually the legal process can help to break complex decisions into a series of simpler choices, within which transitive majority decisions can be reached.[54]

Without a meaningful way to break the decision and avoid the Condorcet Paradox, there is no longer a justification to use emerging consensus. This doesn't mean that the ECHR should always defer to state policies in cases of this kind. The ECHR can and should use other

supporters (some of them located in states such as Florida and Virginia that can determine election results since they shift from Democrat to Republican). See Harry J. Enten, *Felon Voting Rights Have a Bigger Impact on Elections than Voter ID Laws*, THE GUARDIAN July 31, 2013, Available at: www.theguardian.com/commentisfree/2013/jul/31/felon-voting-rights-impact-on-elections .

[54] *See* Lewis A. Kornhauser & Lawrence G. Sager, *Unpacking the Court*, 96 YALE L.J. 82, 107–110 (1986).

doctrines that may lead to a violation finding. In fact, in the *Hirst case* the ECHR decided that the blanket ban on prisoners' right to vote is a violation – regardless of the European consensus – because it indiscriminately restricts a vitally important Convention right.[55]

D What If Judges Misapply Comparative Law?

The analysis so far exposed a series of problems that may occur in the application of emerging consensus due to the behavior of European states. But what if the judges of the ECHR itself misapply emerging consensus? If judges are not properly constrained, they may use emerging consensus in a way that doesn't reflect the decisional benefits of the Jury Theorem.

One way to solve this problem is to try to shape the emerging consensus doctrine in a way that would guide the judges toward its proper use. Guiding judges, however, can prove practically difficult. Another way to solve the problem of misbehaving judges is to try to predict their actual behavior and shape legal procedures in such a way that the best result would ensue. The following subsections investigate these two solutions.

1 The Problems with Guiding Judges

A common argument against the use of comparative law by national courts is that judges do not really try to follow what the majority of states are doing. Instead, judges adopt whatever legal solution they want and later they look for states with similar legal solutions to legitimize their decision.[56] The same argument can easily be targeted against international courts like the ECHR.

In several of its judgments, as illustrated previously, the ECHR actually surveys almost all the states in Europe to provide the judges with an accurate view of the policies adopted by the majority of the states. Because this policy is so entrenched in the ECHR and is done with some precision, the chances that the ECHR will deliberately misrepresent the majority's view in Europe are smaller than in other international courts. Nevertheless, it is difficult to present the laws of states on complex legal

[55] Hirst case, Note 48 at par. 82.

[56] *See* Justice Scalia's dissent in Lawrence v. Texas, 539 U.S. 558, 598 (2003). *See also* Posner & Sunstein, Note 1, Chapter 1 at 139.

issues in a way that is accurate and transparent enough to convince readers that the court used emerging consensus correctly.

In other international courts that do not have a consistent policy of referring to all the states in the world or in a region, using comparative law gives rise to a dilemma. On the one hand, surveying all the countries in the world is wasteful. The mathematical nature of the Jury Theorem is such that the marginal utility of surveying more states drops quickly after the first few states are reviewed. It is possible to get excellent results by counting a small number of states, especially if there is reason to believe that their laws are better than average.[57] To avoid waste, the court should refer only to a handful of states. On the other hand, when the judges can choose the states they review, there is a possibility that the judge will make a biased choice. Judges may choose the states whose laws they prefer, for whatever reason, instead of giving a fair representation of the states' majority view. To avoid a biased choice of states, it may be better to require judges to survey all the states in the world or in the region.

Assuming judges can be trusted not to choose countries in a biased way, judges should choose a small number of states to avoid wasting resources. The best results would naturally come when the judges choose the states with the best laws and follow the majority within this select group. But what are the states with the best laws?

Democratic countries make their laws based on majoritarian institutions that are improved by an additional system of checks and balances. Decisions by majority vote should enjoy the decisional advantages of the Jury Theorem, which would suggest that democratic countries make better policies than non-democracies.[58] As long as democratic processes function appropriately, a bigger country aggregates the collective wisdom of more voters, which would allow it to make better decisions. Having said that, it is important to note both that democratic processes rarely work perfectly and that if the process is perfect, the Jury Theorem would lead to good results even with a small pool of voters. Nevertheless, more populated countries may possess more complex and more expensive systems of aggregating decisions that may lead to better results on the whole.

[57] *See* Posner & Sunstein, Note 1, Chapter 1 at 169. Consider the numerical example in Note 4 for a simple illustration.

[58] *Id*, at 159.

Posner and Sunstein have another suggestion for choosing the states whose laws should be surveyed. They argue that states which serve their citizens well should be given priority over states whose citizens are in a worse condition.[59] There are several problems with this suggestion. First, even if there are good ways to rate states according to the quality of life they give to their citizens, it is often impossible to determine whether this quality of life stems from the state's policy choices and not from other factors such as the state's history or the natural resources it possesses. Second, there are many determinants of quality of life and no way to know which one is more important. Does a state with a high GDP make better policies than a state whose population has a higher life expectancy, or, alternatively, a state with a happier population? Finally, if international courts pick and choose certain states because they believe their laws are better than those of other states, how can these courts still appear objective. The legitimacy of international courts relies to a great extent on their impartiality. Rating states based on the general quality of their regime could seriously jeopardize international courts' legitimacy. For all these reasons, focusing on a limited number of high-quality states seems impossible to execute in a systematic and transparent way.

Another factor international courts may decide to consider is the level of public deliberation that preceded the choice of policy in different states. As subsection 3.C.5 explained, some states simply didn't change their policy and their laws are settled by default. These countries should not be relied on. But the same logic would imply that countries that didn't allocate resources to carefully discuss their policies may be given less weight when international courts conduct an investigation of comparative law or use the emerging consensus doctrine.

2 *Assuming Judges Behave According to Theories of Judicial Behavior*

It may prove very difficult to constrain judges to apply emerging consensus correctly. Monitoring how judges survey the laws of all European states may be an impossible task. If that is the case, one may have to accept the fact that judges have their own goals and they follow them instead of applying the emerging consensus doctrine. But this doesn't

[59] *Id*, at 174–175.

mean that all hope is lost. Predicting how judges are likely to behave would help in tailoring procedural solutions that could lead to good outcomes taking judicial behavior into account.

The literature on judicial behavior developed theories that can help predict how judges are likely to act. This literature is divided to three main models:[60]

(1) *legalist models* – judges try to implement the law itself in their judgments.
(2) *attitudinal models* – judges decide sincerely based on their policy preferences.
(3) *strategic models* – judges try to promote their preferences strategically, taking into account the possible reactions of other actors.

The following subsections offer pragmatic solutions to make the best out of the emerging consensus doctrine, assuming that judges follow each of these models of judicial behavior.

Legalist Judges

According to the legalist model, judges are constrained by the law and apply it accurately, or at least try to do so to the best of their abilities.[61] The legalist model would suggest that judges in the ECHR are constrained by the Convention, but the Convention doesn't say a word about emerging consensus. The emerging consensus doctrine was developed in the court's case law and clarified by it. It is not the only doctrine used by the court, however. Other doctrines and different interpretations of the Convention can draw the court in different directions. If a legalist judge sees the law as something different than emerging consensus, she will apply the law as she sees it and forfeit the decisional advantage of emerging consensus.

Fortunately, this problem has an easy solution. Legalist judges are readily constrained. If the Convention were amended to include a direct requirement to apply emerging consensus, legalist judges would always apply the doctrine. Furthermore, while judges in the ECHR are not formally constrained by precedent, they usually follow their previous

[60] *See* JEFFREY A. SEGAL & HAROLD J. SPAETH, THE SUPREME COURT AND THE ATTITUDINAL MODEL REVISITED 44–114 (2002).

[61] Howard Gillman, *What's Law Got to Do with It?: Judicial Behavioralists Test the "Legal Model" of Judicial Decision Making*, 26 L. & SOC. INQUIRY 465, 485–86 (2001).

judgments unless they have good reason to decide otherwise.[62] Legalist judges who feel a commitment to previous judgments are more likely to apply emerging consensus correctly the more it is clarified and entrenched in the court's judgments.

Attitudinal Judges

According to the attitudinal model, judges decide in line with their policy preferences in a sincere way. This means that judges do not change their decisions based on what they think other judges or actors out of the court will do.[63] Attitudinal judges are not easily constrained by the law. One must either take the preferences of judges as a given and build procedures that can lead to good decisions with that in mind, or change the way judges are selected so that judges with other preferences will sit on the court.

In the ECHR, most of the power to select judges is given to the states. Each state has to present a list with three candidates out of which one judge is selected by the European Parliamentary Assembly.[64] The system already in place may be used to lead to good results according to the Jury Theorem logic. Under the reasonable assumption that states select judges who share their policy views, at least on major issues, the policies favored by the majority of the judges on the ECHR would mirror the policies that are favored by the majority of states in Europe. While it is unlikely that all states can find a judge that sees eye to eye with them on every policy issue, a similarity between the views of the judge and the country that selected her is only to be expected. This implies that a majority vote among all the judges in the ECHR would track the view of most European states and enjoy the advantages of the Jury Theorem.

The only problem is that the ECHR doesn't make its decisions in a full bench. Judgments are issued by panels, mostly Chambers of seven judges and Grand Chambers of seventeen judges.[65] Mathematically speaking,

[62] *Goodwin* case, *supra* Note 39 at 26.

[63] Segal & Spaeth, *supra* Note 60 at 86.

[64] Convention, art. 22. It is important to note, however, that the creation of an advisory panel of experts monitoring the selection of judges for the ECHR may have decreased the ability of states to push through candidates for political reasons, *see* Resolution CM/Res (2010)26 on the Establishment of an Advisory Panel of Experts on Candidates for Election as Judge to the European Court of Human Rights; Shai Dothan, *The Motivations of Individual Judges and How They Act as a Group*, 19 German L.J. 2165, 2168 (2018).

[65] Convention, art. 26(1).

the larger the panel – provided that the judges in it are selected arbitrarily – the higher the probability that the panel decision would be the same as a majority vote among all the judges in the court, which, in turn, is in line with the majority view in Europe.[66] To better track the majority of European states and enjoy the benefits of the Jury Theorem, the ECHR should therefore move more of its important decisions from Chambers to the larger Grand Chambers.

Strategic Judges

Strategic judges are also committed to policy goals. But unlike attitudinal judges, they try to pursue these goals while responding to potential reactions by other judges or institutional actors. The strategic judge will decide in a way that doesn't reflect her sincere preferences, if doing so would lead to a result favorable in her view.[67] Imagine a strategic judge who wants states in Europe to change their laws in accordance with emerging consensus. If the judge suspects that issuing a judgment that accurately tracks the emerging consensus would only result in noncompliance, she may choose to compromise. The judge may issue a judgment that digresses somewhat from emerging consensus, but is likely to be complied with, leading the state to adopt policies that are as similar to emerging consensus as the judge can hope for under current political conditions.

This compromise is problematic. It resigns to the fact that the state before the court will not follow emerging consensus, but only come close to it. Worse still, the judgment will give bad guidance to all the rest of the states in Europe by depicting a biased version of emerging consensus. Other states may be misled and adopt suboptimal policies.

A strategic judge will decide exactly in accordance with her policy preferences if she can be convinced that her judgment will be complied with. If the goal of the strategic judge is to have states behave in accordance with emerging consensus, she will require them to do just that as long as compliance is assured. If states can expect a significant reputational sanction for noncompliance with the ECHR,[68] or, alternatively, if the Committee of Ministers develops an effective mechanism to

[66] *See* Menachem Mautner, *Luck in Courts*, 9 Theo. Inq. L. 217, 224 (2007).

[67] *See* Lee Epstein, Jack Knight, & Andrew D. Martin, *The Political (Science) Context of Judging*, 47 St. Louis U. L.J. 783, 798 (2003).

[68] I investigated the ways national and international courts can increase the reputational sanctions imposed on noncompliant states in Dothan, Note 3, Chapter 1.

ensure compliance with the court's judgments, the chances of compliance go up. The higher the probability of compliance, the more likely it is that strategic judges will apply emerging consensus correctly, knowing that states are likely to follow their judgments and adjust domestic policies accordingly. Therefore, the proper cure for the biases of strategic judges – of the specific kind discussed here – is to increase the likelihood that states will comply with ECHR judgments.

E Conclusion

This chapter argued that international courts sometimes possess a unique advantage over national courts. International courts can use comparative law to follow the policies adopted by the majority of states in the world or in a region, without falling into information cascades. If states adopt their policies independently, the policy supported by the majority of the states is likely to be correct according to the Condorcet Jury Theorem. The emerging consensus doctrine can help find the policy that serves best the interests of everyone in the region under conditions of uncertainty.

The emerging consensus doctrine is applied by the ECHR, although it isn't mentioned in the Convention. The previous chapter argued that under certain circumstances the ECHR may be justified in using expansive interpretation to read into the Convention provisions that do not clearly appear in the text. As long as the text itself doesn't contradict the interpretation given by the court and there is reason to believe that the treaty misrepresents the will of the state parties or that states parties misrepresent the people affected by the treaty, the court can use teleological interpretation to accomplish the object and purpose of the Convention.

The purpose of the Convention, broadly put, is to improve the protection of human rights. What better way to do that than to follow policies that are calculated to best serve the interests of all people in countries subject to the Convention? One way to understand the emerging consensus doctrine therefore is as a sophisticated method to assess the hypothetical will of all the people affected by the Convention. The argument presented in this chapter suggests that emerging consensus may help find the best policies from the perspective of everyone involved. When the actual wishes of everyone are not manifested in the text of the Convention due to democratic failures, this may by the optimal technique to serve the hypothetical will of the peoples of Europe. Serving this hypothetical will would accomplish the purpose of the Convention.

4

Why International Courts Improve Deliberation

Up to this point, the book has argued that international courts can sometimes intervene legitimately in domestic affairs and that they can sometimes make better decisions than domestic bodies. But critics of international courts may still be unsatisfied. They would argue that international courts make decisions without an open public debate. Deliberation is the essence of democracy, they would say, and closing the public out of the discussion by issuing a final judgment is unacceptable.[1] An improved policy isn't worth that sacrifice.

Those critics are right about the importance of deliberation, but they are wrong about what international courts do. An international judgment isn't the end of the discussion. It is often just the beginning of a dialogue with the public and its representatives. International courts do not stop public deliberation. They can strengthen and improve it. This chapter explains why.

The chapter first describes how international courts involve the public in deliberating over policy issues. It illustrates how international courts motivate the public to get involved and provide the public with the legal terms that facilitate their deliberation. Later, the chapter analyzes the responses of the three domestic branches of government – the executive branch, the legislative branch, and the judicial branch – to international courts. The friction between international courts and these governmental branches invigorates public deliberation. Finally, the chapter demonstrates how international courts build a global elite of lawyers that push forward the public debate in their own countries and transnationally.

[1] *See e.g.* Lord Sumption, The 27th Sultan Azlan Shah Lecture, Kuala Lumpur: The Limits of Law, 9–15 (Nov. 20, 2013), www.supremecourt.uk/docs/speech-131120.pdf.

A Stirring the General Public

1 The Myth of International Courts

Several years ago, a few youngsters launched a viral internet campaign called "Kony 2012." The campaign started with a half hour YouTube clip[2] that called on the public to get involved and pressure their governments to arrest militia leader Joseph Kony. The clip accumulated more than 100 million views by 2016. All over the world, people hanged posters and drew graffiti advocating the capture of Kony.

This unprecedented wave of public engagement would not have been possible if it wasn't for the ICC. The ICC indicted Kony and raised awareness of his crimes. Far more importantly, it created an image that there is a respectable international forum where Kony can receive a fair trial and be brought to justice.

Unfortunately, this image is still more a myth than reality. In 2019, Kony is still a fugitive and the ICC managed to convict only eight people in more than sixteen years. While most courts draw their strength from public knowledge and awareness, the ICC is powerful because people are ignorant. The public believes that the ICC is a major player in world politics. They do not know how slow, how expensive, and how scarce are proceedings before the court. This is the true source of the ICC's influence.

To get the public involved in politics one needs to have a rallying cry. The myth of international courts can provide this cry. When the newspapers are full of stories about the ICC, even hardened soldiers start looking over their shoulder. They will be deterred even if they find nobody there. This phenomenon isn't unique to the ICC. People in Russia need to believe that the ECHR offers some protection of their rights. Their belief changes the way they behave and shapes reality. The ICJ has cultivated a myth that it is the forum where states should settle their disputes, and this myth is essential for the preservation of world peace.

For the myth of international courts to succeed, people need to know these courts exist and to be interested in them, but they do not need to know too many details. Research shows that people google the ECHR and the CJEU quite often, and they can read about these courts in the popular press. It is rather embarrassing that many newspapers mistake

2 www.youtube.com/watch?v=Y4MnpzG5Sqc.

one of these courts for the other.[3] This mistake is also dangerous – many people who voted for Brexit may have thought it would absolve them from the ECHR's scrutiny, not realizing that the United Kingdom would still be under the court's jurisdiction even if it leaves the European Union.[4] But despite the inaccuracies in public perception of international courts, these courts are salient in people's minds and this can motivate people to action.

Motivating people to action is the key to having an informed public and to sustaining true democratic deliberation. Doing this is very hard because it goes against people's egotistical interests. Every rational individual has a powerful incentive to invest her energy in things that improve her own well-being. When I invest hours in researching what cell-phone to buy, I know that I will reap the fruits of my effort alone. I won't have to share these benefits with anybody. In contrast, when I consider whether to read about human rights abuses in my country, or in my continent, I must understand that any advantages gained from my actions will be spread across millions of people I know nothing about. Most people would make the rational choice and keep out of politics.[5]

Who stands to gain from this predicament? Scholars have shown that small and well-organized interest groups can use the indifference of the public to accumulate great power and influence.[6] In fact, small interest groups enrich themselves at the expense of the public to such an extent that they can stifle economic growth.[7] The public can stop these interest groups only if it is properly informed.

This is the task of international courts – to raise public awareness and prevent society from being fooled by a small and exploitative elite. The myth of international courts spurs the public to act: to litigate, to lobby, or simply to learn more about their rights. International courts often lack the resources and the political clout to force the hand of society's rulers, but they can marshal the public to oppose their rule by giving people clear targets and accessible information.

[3] *See* Voeten, Note 73, Chapter 2 at 419–422.

[4] *See* Tim Worstall, *Misunderstanding Brexit – Scrapping The Human Rights Act for a British Bill of Rights*, FORBES Aug. 23, 2016.

[5] *See* BRUCE ACKERMAN & JAMES FISHKIN, DELIBERATION DAY 8 (2004).

[6] *See* OLSON, Note 86, Chapter 2 at 33–34; Lohmann, Note 87, Chapter 2 at 812; Ackerman, Note 85, Chapter 2 at 724.

[7] *See* MANCUR OLSON, THE RISE AND DECLINE OF NATIONS: ECONOMIC GROWTH, STAGFLATION, AND SOCIAL RIGIDITIES 74 (1982).

2 *Changing the Discourse from Interests to Rights*

Judges are experts in recognizing legal rights. Their mission is to turn a story about conflicting interests into a reasoned judgment. This involves applying vague legal provisions to the facts. It involves naming specific violations of rights and balancing between those rights. Courts are repeating the facts in their judgments, but they are telling a special kind of story. A story about rights, not about interests.

One of the key impacts that courts have on society is changing the public debate to resemble the kind of story that judges are telling. Courts are transforming the way people argue. They turn a debate about political power into a discussion about principles and values.[8] By applying public values to concrete situations, judges are giving content and depth to these values and provide the necessary tools for a principled public discourse.[9]

The transformation of public discourse was the traditional task of national courts, mainly courts of last resort. In recent years, international courts are starting to share this burden and shape the deliberation of the public worldwide. Ideas that appear in international judgments have an impact far beyond the formal jurisdiction of the courts that issued them. One way to demonstrate this phenomenon is by studying national courts that cite international judgments to which they are not legally bound. International courts do not have a legal effect on these national courts, but they form principles that shape the way national judges reason. The same principles that appear in the discussions of judges in foreign jurisdictions will pop up in the arguments that shape the political debate. If anything, this effect will be stronger the closer one gets to the international court's jurisdiction.

One of the principles that was promoted by the CJEU and influenced the discourse all over the world is "equal pay for equal work." CJEU judgments have viewed differences in payment for women and men as suspected of unlawful discrimination unless the difference is justified by objective reasons. A dissent written by Judge Michal Kirby of the High Court of Australia in the case of *New South Wales* v. *Amery* shows how far the principles developed in Europe have reached. Kirby interprets the Australian Anti-Discrimination Act in light of CJEU judgments.

[8] *See* Frank I. Michelman, *The Constitution, Social Rights, and Liberal Political Justification*, 1 I-CON, 13, 34 (2003).

[9] *See* Owen M. Fiss, *Foreword: The Forms of Justice*, 93 HARV. L. REV. 1, 29–30 (1979); Owen M. Fiss, *The Social and Political Foundations of Adjudication*, 6 LAW & HUM. BEHAV. 121, 125 (1982).

Specifically, he asserted that Australian courts should be willing to intervene when employers set unreasonable requirements that discriminate between men and women.[10] Although Kirby's opinion didn't convince the majority in this case, it powerfully demonstrates the impact of the CJEU on principles that are applied outside its jurisdiction.

Even the United States Supreme Court – famous for its policy of American exceptionalism – is not immune from the influence of principles developed by international courts to which it is not formally bound. An example is the judgment of Justice Kennedy in *Lawrence* v. *Texas*.[11] Kennedy delivered the opinion of the court that decided to overrule a recent precedent of the Supreme Court, *Bowers* v. *Hardwick*,[12] which ruled that the criminalization of sodomy is constitutional. *Bowers* v. *Hardwick* included a concurring judgment by Justice Burger that asserted that criminalizing homosexual conduct is common within Western civilization.[13] In order to disprove this assertion and show that many Western countries do not criminalize homosexuality, Justice Kennedy refers[14] to the ECHR case of *Dudgeon* v. *United Kingdom*.[15] This famous case ruled that criminalizing homosexual sex between consenting adults is in violation of the European Convention on Human Rights. While it is clear that the reference to the ECHR doesn't show any commitment to follow the ECHR's judgments, it demonstrates that moral principles developed by this international court shape the discourse far beyond its jurisdiction.

Another case where principles developed by the ECHR had an effect outside its jurisdiction is the Israeli judgment that prohibited the use of several interrogation techniques on suspected terrorists. One of the techniques forbidden by the judgment of the Israeli Supreme Court was called "Shabach." People subjected to this technique were handcuffed and seated on a very low chair. Their head was covered with a bag and they had to stay in a room with noisy music.[16] The Israeli court referred to the ECHR judgment of *Ireland* v. *United Kingdom*, which decided that

[10] The State of New South Wales v. Amery and Others, [2006] HCA 14 par. 168–171.
[11] Lawrence v. Texas, 539 U.S. 558 (2003).
[12] Bowers v. Hardwick, 478 U.S. 186 (1986).
[13] *Id* at 196.
[14] Lawrence v. Texas, at 572–573.
[15] Dudgeon v. The United Kingdom, judgment of October 22, 1981 EUR. Ct. H.R. (ser. A) 45.
[16] HCJ 5100/94 Public Committee against Torture v. Israel [1999] IsrSC 53(4) 817, at par. 26, 30 to the judgment of the President Aharon Barak.

similar interrogation techniques violated the European Convention on Human Rights as they constituted "inhuman and degrading treatment."[17] The Israeli court adopted the moral standards promoted by an international court, without legal commitment to do so.

These examples demonstrate that international courts can frame the debate even when their judgments are not legally binding. Just like judges in foreign jurisdictions used moral principles developed by international courts in their arguments, members of the public can do the same. In this way, international courts are not only securing more democratic deliberation. They are improving the debate by framing it as an issue of rights and principles.

3 *Acting as a Stage to Disseminate Information*

International courts do not exist in a social vacuum. They are surrounded by NGOs, lawyers, and activists that collaborate with the courts and help them fulfill their goals. This phenomenon may have harmful side effects, as discussed in Chapter 5, but it helps international courts disseminate information about their agenda to the general public. While traditional international courts like the ICJ are relatively elitist institutions, approached only by a small group of litigators,[18] international courts like the ECHR or the IACHR maintain numerous points of contact with the public at large.

NGOs that collaborate with the ECHR – writing amicus curiae briefs, publishing information on the court, or monitoring compliance with its judgments – are forming a large community that surrounds the court's officials. To borrow terms from Social Network Analysis, this community can be called a "periphery," which surrounds the "core" of professionals within the court. Social Network Analysis is a sociological methodology that can help assess, among other things, how information flows in networks of individuals or organizations. The network structure around the ECHR includes a small core of densely connected professionals and a large periphery of activists that are not densely connected to one another, but form connections to the core. This network structure is ideal for facilitating the flow of information in the network as a whole.

[17] Case of Ireland v. The United Kingdom, judgment of January 18, 1978 at par. 167.

[18] *See* Sara Dezalay & Yves Dezalay, *Professionals of International Justice: From the Shadow of State Diplomacy to the Pull of the Market for Commercial Arbitration, in* International Law as a Profession 311, 320 (eds. Jean D'Aspremont et al, 2017).

A powerful demonstration of the way this network structure serves the flow of information actually comes from a study on the epidemiology of sexually transmitted diseases. Research shows that social groups with a densely connected core – namely, people with many sexual partners – who connect to a large periphery of people with only a few sexual partners, spread diseases very quickly throughout society at large. This type of network is known as "dissortative mixing." Networks of this kind spread diseases much faster than networks where the core and the periphery have only a few connections.[19] Information and sexually transmitted diseases behave essentially the same way. The core of elite professionals around the court change the law, elaborate on moral principles, and create ideas. These ideas are then communicated to the periphery of lawyers and activists that spread it around very quickly. The connections between the core and the periphery ensure a rapid dissemination of information to a much larger social group.

As Chapter 5 shows, the ECHR is starting to rely more and more on NGOs for monitoring compliance with its judgments. This is the privilege of a court with hundreds of important cases each year and a high compliance rate. The IACHR isn't quite there yet. It has to struggle with prevalent noncompliance and a region rife with severe problems. Research shows that the IACHR adapted to that unfortunate situation by transforming into a stage where the public can witness important cases being argued. The court is focusing not only on direct compliance with its judgments. It is trying to initiate social processes with long-term implications by exposing the public to new information.

Some of the actions of the IACHR can only be explained with a view to its unique role as a source of information. When a state accepts responsibility for its actions, the IACHR will not seize this opportunity to close the case as quickly as possible. Instead, it will initiate long days of hearings, collect evidence from witnesses, and analyze the relevant facts.[20] The court clearly isn't trying to affect direct compliance, given that the state has already admitted a violation. It is trying to process and disseminate as much information as possible. The hope is that an

19 *See* Edward O. Laumann & Yoosik Youm, *Racial/Ethnic Group Differences in the Prevalence of Sexually Transmitted Diseases in the United States: A Network Explanation*, 26 Sexually Transmitted Diseases 250 (1999).

20 *See* James L. Cavallaro & Stephanie Erin Brewer, *Reevaluating Regional Human Rights Litigation in the Twenty-First Century: The Case of the Inter-American Court*, 102 Am. J. Int'l. L. 768, 808–816 (2008).

informed public will eventually change the way states in the region behave.

All this indicates that international courts are able to change the views of the public even when they cannot enforce their judgments directly. Does this imply that international courts can also initiate social change? Some scholars believe that every member of the public can exert a small influence that changes society from the bottom up.[21] According to this view, the impact that international courts have on the masses will translate to a potent effect on the way states behave. International courts do not just push forward public deliberation – this deliberation can make a real difference.

The interactions between states were traditionally seen as the province of diplomats: direct representatives of the tip of the governments' hierarchy.[22] In contrast, today more and more interactions are taking place between lower levels of the states' governance. Judges, generals, bankers – they all form connections that cross national borders.[23] These bureaucrats may now be able to shape policy unconstrained by formal international law.[24] But they are affected by the public, and the public is informed and organized by international courts.

B A Dialogue with Governments

The literature on international courts has long realized that these courts are constrained institutions. International courts are limited by the treaties that form them and the type of judgments they are legally capable of issuing. In addition, international courts are threatened with the use of several political countermeasures that range from exiting the court's jurisdiction to failing to comply with its judgments. International courts that are aware of these political constraints would shape their judgments so that they can avoid a dangerous backlash.[25]

[21] *See* Harold Hongju Koh, *How Is International Human Rights Law Enforced?* 74 Ind. L.J. 1397, 1416 (1999).

[22] *See* Benvenisti, Exit and Voice in the Age of Globalization, Note 85, Chapter 2 at 184–186.

[23] *See* Anne-Marie Slaughter, A New World Order (2004).

[24] *See* Joost Pauwelyn, Ramses A. Wessel, & Jan Wouters, *An Introduction to Informal International Lawmaking, in* Informal International Lawmaking 1, 3 (Joost Pauwelyn, Ramses A. Wessel, & Jan Wouters, eds., 2012).

[25] *See* Dothan, Note 3, Chapter 1 at 87–101.

This section isn't concerned with limits on the court's discretion or with reprisals that can dictate the type of decisions courts make. It is focused on mechanisms that come into play once the court issues a judgment, mechanisms which are intended to limit or to change the impact of this judgment itself on society. International courts are not simply issuing orders. They are engaging in a dialogue with political bodies. The response of the executive, the legislator, and the judiciary will determine how much of the court's judgment is implemented on the ground. More importantly for the purpose of this chapter, the response of these political bodies shapes the court's impact on public deliberation. The following subsections argue that the dialogue between international courts and the branches of government is conducive to a vibrant public deliberation.

1 The Executive

The executive is the main body charged with implementing international judgments. Often, the executive will resist such judgments and limit their effectiveness. Scholars that have studied the CJEU argue that despite its undeniable impact on the European Union, it can only shape policy after a political struggle. A CJEU judgment is only the beginning of a dialogue. If the judgment is to affect policy, it must be followed by mobilization of the public that would push the executive to comply with the court's judgment. One case isn't enough either. The public would have to initiate many similar CJEU cases before policies in Europe gradually begin to change.[26]

Take the ECJ's famous *Cassis* decision,[27] which ruled that goods that are produced and marketed lawfully in one European state can be lawfully sold all over the European Union.[28] When the decision was issued, it was, at first, all but ignored by member states. That is only to be expected. After all, the decision attempted to push forward European integration by encroaching on state sovereignty. But then the European Commission got involved and endeavored to set policy in accordance

[26] *See* Lisa J. Conant, Justice Contained: Law and Politics in the European Union 32–38 (2002). Compare Schmidt, Note 2, Chapter 3 at 238 (suggesting, in contrast, that EU case law is often implemented, at least by the administration of Western member states).

[27] Rewe Zentrale AG v. Bundesmonopolverwaltung für Branntwein C-120/78, (1979) European court Reports (E.C.R.), 649.

[28] *See* Conant, Note 26 at 1–2.

with the ECJ's judgment. States naturally resisted and the public became mobilized. Interest groups were marshaled to fight either for or against the ECJ's judgment. The ultimate result of this struggle was a compromise solution that gave states a limited ability to control their internal regulation with no external influence.[29]

The *Cassis* decision was implemented after substantial delay, and only in part. But imagine how much deliberation followed the ECJ's decision, how much deliberation became possible because of the judgment of an international court. The role of the ECJ in this story is mainly to set focal points for the coordination of contrasting political movements.[30] International courts help members of the public to realize that they have a common interest and that they can argue for this interest collectively. International judgments help to crystallize the debate by pointing out the main issues of contention.[31]

Creating friction between social groups and the government is the classical role of national courts. By making the actions of governments known and subject to scrutiny, courts can involve wider segments of the public in political deliberation. This, in turn, decreases the ability of small interest groups to capture the government and to take advantage of most of the public.[32] International courts like the CJEU are increasingly assuming the same role.

The CJEU relies on public participation not only for the enforcement of its judgments. It also uses the public as a method to expose itself to new cases. There are three channels that bring cases to the CJEU: (1) national courts making preliminary references on questions of EU law; (2) an infringement procedure by the Commission based on a complaint issued by an individual or a NGO; (3) an infringement procedure that the Commission issued based on its own initiative. Around 2006, the number of cases initiated by the Commission started to decrease precipitously while the number of cases beginning with preliminary references from national courts increased. Furthermore, the number of complaints

29 *See id* at 11–14.

30 *See* David S. Law, *A Theory of Judicial Power and Judicial Review*, 97 Geo. L.J. 723, 759–762 (2009).

31 Tom Ginsburg & Richard H. McAdams, *Adjudication in Anarchy: An Expressive Theory of International Dispute Resolution*, 45 Wm & Mary L. Rev. 1229, 1275 (2004).

32 *See* Benvenisti, Judicial Review and Democratic Failures, Note 85, Chapter 2.

received by the Commission remains high and has been increasing since 2012.[33]

The Commission has adopted a "fire alarm" instead of a "police patrol" model for supervising violations by states. The Commission issues fewer and fewer cases on its own initiative. Instead, the Commission waits for people either to bring cases to it by filing a complaint or to start a proceeding before national courts that may lead to a preliminary reference to the CJEU. The main advantage of the "fire alarm" model is that it saves costs for the central regulator and lets the public do most of the work.[34] This model for monitoring violations gives the public an opportunity and an incentive to get involved. With more and more members of the public engaged in exposing violations of EU law, public deliberation can flourish.

2 *The Legislator*

By changing legislation at the right time, parliaments can save their countries a finding of violation by an international court. International courts cast a double effect on parliaments: They expand their agenda by leading to more legislation and they change the way parliaments deliberate and justify their legislation.

A good example of a change of agenda instigated by an international court is the way the ICC set in motion numerous legislative efforts in the field of international criminal law. The ICC adopted a rule of complementarity that prevents it from prosecuting suspected war criminals if they were investigated or prosecuted in a country that is both willing and able to conduct prosecution itself. In order to show that their country is willing and able to conduct international trials for war criminals, many parliaments had to revise and expand their country's criminal codes. They had to define a new set of international crimes that fits the ones mentioned in the Rome Statute – the founding treaty of the ICC.[35] In this way, the ICC put a thorny topic on the agenda of

[33] *See* Andreas Hofmann, *Is the Commission Levelling the Playing Field? Rights Enforcement in the European Union*, 40 J. Eur. Integration 737, 739–741 (2018).

[34] *Id* at 740–741, Mathew D. McCubbins & Thomas Scwartz, *Congressional Oversight Overlooked: Police Patrols versus Fire Alarms*, 28 Amer. J. Pol. Sci. 165, 168 (1984).

[35] *See* Jann K. Kleffner, Complementarity in the Rome Statute and National Criminal Jurisdictions 333–337 (2008).

parliaments and initiated a healthy public debate about the issue of prosecuting war criminals.

The second effect on the practice of parliaments has to do with the actual deliberation within them. Scholars have investigated the way international courts like the CJEU change the nature of discussions that take place in the legislator. Parliaments are subject to potential judicial challenges before the CJEU and this doesn't only change the type of issues about which they legislate. It also changes the way they reason. Members of the legislator are trying to preempt judicial challenges by using traditional judicial techniques such as balancing and tests of proportionality. Over time, parliaments are internalizing the principles and the types of arguments that are prevalent in international courts.[36]

The combination of these two factors is especially powerful. International courts are responsible both for initiating discussions that would otherwise not take place and for shaping parliamentary discussions as a debate about abstract rights instead of crude interests. In this way, international courts improve deliberation between the chief representatives of the public. These deliberations are usually covered by the media and are therefore likely to raise awareness within the public as well.

3 *The Judiciary*

As mentioned previously, national courts are useful for limiting the power of small interest groups and allowing larger parts of the public to participate in politics. At the same time, national courts can also protect their countries from foreign influence, which is sometimes even more inimical to public deliberation. International courts can improve the cooperation of national courts, making national courts more immune to political pressures from their governments and enabling them to fulfill their important role.

National courts used to shy away from applying international law because it was considered a threat to their countries' interests.[37] But in recent years, national courts are doing exactly the opposite. Realizing that foreign pressures are damaging their countries more than compliance

[36] *See* ALEC STONE SWEET, GOVERNING WITH JUDGES: CONSTITUTIONAL POLITICS IN EUROPE 204 (2000).

[37] *See* Eyal Benvenisti, *Judicial Misgivings Regarding the Application of International Law: An Analysis of Attitudes of National Courts*, 4 EUR. J. INT'L. L. 159, 167 (1993).

with international law, national courts are applying more international law in their judgments.[38]

International law is used as a tool. It can help shield states from foreign pressures by giving them an ability to commit to certain policies. Counterintuitively, states fare better when they are constrained by international law because this immunizes them from harmful influences.[39] The problem with the use of this tool is that national courts may be subject to such pressure from their governments that they would not be able to effectively constrain the government for its own good. Scholars have argued that national courts across the world can cooperate with each other to increase their resistance to political pressures.[40]

This is where international courts come into the picture. Scholars have pointed out that international courts can coordinate the actions of national courts and help them unite against the forces that attempt to constrain them. For example, the CJEU fulfilled this role vis-à-vis the national courts of Belgium and the Netherlands. As the courts of relatively small European countries, the Belgian and Dutch courts witnessed their countries pressed by some of the bigger economies in the continent. They realized that the CJEU can be their ally in securing European policies that suit their countries' interests. Scholars argued that this is why these two countries referred so many cases to the CJEU, despite their small populations, giving the CJEU the opportunity to become an influential actor in Europe.[41]

When countries are squeezed by foreign powers, domestic deliberation is curtailed. The public is left out of the important political decisions, which are directed by other states. These states are, in turn, often directed by small interest groups that determine their foreign policy. It is the task of national courts to make these powers visible to the public and to allow the domestic society to resist them.[42]

But sometimes foreign influence doesn't stem from other states. It can also come directly from international organizations. The United Nations

[38] *See* Eyal Benvenisti, *Reclaiming Democracy: The Strategic Uses of Foreign and International Law by National Courts*, 102 AMER. J. INT'L L. 241 (2008).

[39] *See id* at 248.

[40] *See* Eyal Benvenisti & George W. Downs, *National Courts, Domestic Democracy, and the Evolution of International Law*, 20 EUR. J. INT'L L. 59, 65 (2009).

[41] *See* Eyal Benvenisti & George W. Downs, *The Premises, Assumptions and Implications of* Van Gend en Loos: *Viewed from the Perspectives of Democracy and Legitimacy of International Institutions*, 25 EUR. J. INT'L L. 85, 92–93 (2014).

[42] *See id* at 95.

Security Council, controlled by a handful of global powers, can force states to change their domestic policies. The famous *Kadi* cases demonstrate how an international court, the CJEU, can protect states from such intervention.

The *Kadi* cases dealt with a suspected member of Al-Qaeda. The Security Council subjected him to several sanctions that included the freezing of his assets. In the *first Kadi* case, the CJEU decided that because the suspect didn't receive a proper hearing, the EU regulation that followed the Security Council's resolution and limited his rights must be annulled.[43] In the *second Kadi* case, the CJEU decided that it can only consider evidence that was revealed to the suspect when assessing the danger he poses to society. Because this evidence wasn't enough – according to the CJEU – to justify the sanctions against him, they too were annulled.[44]

The *Kadi* cases aid public deliberation in two levels of abstraction. First, they allow European countries to prevent foreign intervention in their domestic policies, keeping the European public in charge of defining their own human rights protection. Second, the judgment makes it harder to keep information secret while using it to constrain basic rights of suspects.

National courts often partner with international courts in enforcing international law on recalcitrant governments. But even if national courts do not follow the prescriptions of an international court, the international court may still shape domestic public discourse. Take the *Avena* judgment[45] of the ICJ. The ICJ ordered the United States to review the convictions of Mexicans who were sentenced to death, because they were denied their rights under the Vienna Convention on Consular Relations. The American Supreme Court had the final word on the matter, deciding, in the *Medellin* case,[46] that the ICJ judgment should be ignored. Nevertheless, before the Supreme Court issued its judgment, there were powerful domestic forces supporting compliance with the ICJ. In fact, President George W. Bush issued a memorandum directing the Attorney General to comply with the ICJ's judgment. The politicians and social

[43] Case C-402/05P and C-415/05P. Kadi and Al Barakaat International Foundation v. Council and Commission [2008] ECR I-6351.

[44] Case C-584/10P, C-593/10P, and C 595/10P Commission v. Kadi, judgment of July 18, 2013.

[45] Case Concerning Avena and Other Mexican Nationals (Mex. v. U.S.), [2004] ICJ Rep. 12.

[46] Medellin v. Texas, 552 U.S. 491 (2008).

groups that were marshaled in support of the ICJ judgment didn't disappear because of the Supreme Court's judgment. Most likely, they continued to change the domestic political agenda following the initial push by the ICJ.[47]

C An International Network of Lawyers

A debate about international law cannot exist without international lawyers. Only trained professionals have the necessary knowledge to discuss the points of law behind the big policy issues that affect the rest of society. International courts are casting a substantial and increasing effect on the development of the network of international lawyers. They are not only training lawyers directly but they are also the reason so many lawyers are hired by governments, and they have a growing influence on the development of legal academia.

1 International Courts as Social Hubs

Many international courts have flourishing legal-internship programs.[48] These programs give law students and lawyers a first-hand knowledge of the courts' procedures. Lawyers trained in these programs will continue to litigate before international courts in later stages of their professional lives. Just as importantly, they will meet many other international lawyers and build a network of personal connections that will serve them throughout their careers. The global elite of lawyers that grows out of these networks has a substantial impact on domestic discourse as well. For example, the Inter-American Commission on Human Rights, which refers cases to the IACHR, is proud of the fact that many of its past interns defended human rights in their home countries.[49]

In addition to temporary interns, the permanent staff of international courts includes many more people besides the judges. International

[47] I thank W. Michael Reisman for this idea.

[48] *See* the following programs for these respective courts (last visited Jan. 22, 2017): CJEU: http://curia.europa.eu/jcms/jcms/Jo2_7008/traineeships ECHR: www.echr.coe.int/pages/home.aspx?p=employmentandtraineeships&c= IACHR: www.corteidh.or.cr/index.php/en/about-us/programa-pasantias ICC: www.icc-cpi.int/jobs/Pages/internships-and-Visiting-Professionals.aspx ICTY: www.icty.org/en/employment/internships ICTR: http://ictr-archive09.library.cornell.edu/ENGLISH/opportunities/internship/program.html.

[49] *See* www.oas.org/en/iachr/employment/internships.asp (last visited Jan. 22, 2017).

criminal courts have an especially large staff that includes hundreds of professionals. So does the ECHR.[50] These people have a substantial impact on the judgments of the courts in which they work. They will also use their skills and knowledge in later stages of their careers, adding their voice to the elite of lawyers that flourishes thanks to international courts.

Just as important as the people that work inside international courts are the people who work with them – namely, litigators. Many of the litigators before international courts are "repeat players" – they appear before the same court many times. Some people even switch from working at the court to arguing before it as litigators. The final stage in their career may be to become an academic and write about the court they know so well.[51] These people who collaborate repeatedly with international courts tend to adopt the ways of reasoning used in these courts and plant them in the legal and political debates that take place in their home countries.

2 *Motivating Governments to Hire More Lawyers*

International courts are excellent training grounds for lawyers. But they also force governments to train lawyers in order to resist potential legal challenges before them. Lawyers that are recruited to resist the intervention of international courts continue to be active in their own national systems for many more years. The scholarship that studied the role of lawyers in society concluded that lawyers are generally a vital tool in protecting the rule of law and democratic values.[52] The same lawyers that were hired to protect the sovereignty of their countries against international courts will end up promoting democratic deliberation in their countries in later stages of their professional life.

[50] *See* Stéphanie Cartier & Cristina Hoss, *The Role of Registries and Legal Secretariats in International Judicial Institutions, in* The Oxford Handbook of International Adjudication 712, 713–714 (Cesare P. R. Romano et al., eds., 2013).

[51] *See* Antoine Vauchez, *Communities of International Litigators, in* The Oxford Handbook of International Adjudication 655, 657, 661 (Cesare P. R. Romano et al., eds., 2013).

[52] *See* Terence C. Halliday, Lucien Karpik, & Malcolm Feeley, *Introduction – The Legal Complex in Struggles for Political Liberalism, in* Fighting for Political Freedom: Comparative Studies of the Legal Complex and Political Change 1–9 (Terence C. Halliday, Lucien Karpik, & Malcolm Feeley, eds., 2007).

A good example for such a nonintuitive process is the mass recruitment of lawyers to advise militaries around the world in the hope of preempting ICC prosecution. States have formed large cores of advisers and legal experts whose primary aim is to prevent their countries from facing allegations of war crimes.[53] But these lawyers will continue to use their skills and their experience to shape public deliberation in their countries for many years to come.

Some international courts are not satisfied with only this indirect influence on domestic lawyers. The IACHR often directly supervises the criminal process within the states under its jurisdiction, pulling up the quality of their legal systems.[54] This court is so committed to improving domestic legal systems that it sometimes even requires governments to provide legal training to their officials.[55]

3 *Contributing to Legal Academia*

There are many academics that owe their careers to the success of international courts. Research centers focused on international courts are flourishing,[56] and increasingly sophisticated papers about international courts are being published every year.[57] Legal academia, as well as faculties of political science and international relations, are forming a dense network of scholars that write on international courts. This network is a classic "epistemic community" – a social group armed with specialized knowledge, which can use this knowledge to influence policymaking.[58]

The epistemic community of professionals studying international courts is partly responsible for the growing influence of these courts. International judgments are the focus of heated debates between these academics. Scholarly debates trickle down to the discussions in the media

[53] *See* Or Bassok, *Missing in Action: The Human Eye in* Constitutions across Borders in the Struggle against Terrorism 283 (Federico Fabbrini & Vicki Jackson, eds., 2016).

[54] *See* Alexandra Huneeus, *International Criminal Law by Other Means: The Quasi-Criminal Jurisdiction of International Courts*, 107 Am. J. Int'l L. 1, 1–2 (2013).

[55] *See id* at 20–22.

[56] For example, the Centre on International Courts and Tribunals at the University College of London, iCourts at the University of Copenhagen and PluriCourts at the University of Oslo.

[57] *See* Gregory Shaffer & Tom Ginsburg, *The Empirical Turn in International Legal Scholarship*, 106 Am. J. Int'l L. 1, 16–19 (2012).

[58] *See* Peter M. Haas, *Introduction: Epistemic Communities and International Policy Coordination*, 46 Int'l Org. 1, 3 (1992).

and in the general public. In this way, universities are mediating between the doctrinal and policy statements of courts and public deliberation, allowing courts to contribute to that deliberation.

D Conclusion

The goal of this chapter was to argue that international courts are not saying the last word on every policy issue on their agenda. On the contrary, international courts are often the starting point for a healthy public debate. The chapter suggested that international courts are able to shift the focus of the public from fighting over interests to arguing over legal rights. International courts interact with branches of government in ways that spread information to wide segments of the public and involve them in politics. Networks of lawyers and scholars expand thanks to international courts and these networks are crucial for improving the quality of public deliberation.

Nevertheless, even if international courts don't always have the last word, their word has a significant weight. International courts are centers of power and as such they are at risk of being captured by interest groups. These interest groups may work through the intricate web of NGOs that collaborate with international courts. NGOs are proving more and more essential for the success of international courts, but they may want something in return. Are the benefits of NGO intervention worth the risk of capture? The next chapter will attempt to answer this question.

5

Who Should Participate in the Courts' Proceedings?

Just like planets, international courts have satellites. These satellites are known as Non-Governmental Organizations (NGOs) – nonprofit organizations that use their legal expertise to influence policy. NGOs can collaborate with international courts in a variety of ways. They can bring cases to the courts or argue before them. They can lobby for or against a court in international fora. They can also attempt to enforce a court's judgment after it was issued.

The moon is a natural satellite that rotates around the earth. It is so massive that it affects the tides of our seas. A similar danger may lurk for international courts. Some of their more potent satellites – large and professional NGOs – may exert an influence on the content of their judgments. Powerful NGOs cost a lot of money, giving the rich an unfair advantage in capturing international courts to do their will. After presenting the methods that NGOs can use to collaborate with international courts, this chapter will try to assess the costs and benefits of this collaboration. NGOs can lead to many advantages and these must be remembered when setting the procedures that regulate their appearances before international courts.

The course of an object leaving the earth's atmosphere may shift due to the gravitational forces of the earth's satellites. Similarly, when a judgment is issued by an international court, its ultimate social impact depends on the forces exerted by NGOs. Would the debate between numerous NGOs that shame states for violations exposed by an international court get international public opinion closer or further away from the truth? This question is addressed by an empirical study whose results are described later on in this chapter.

A How Can NGOs Participate?

The methods of collaboration between an international court and a NGO can be divided into three types: (1) formal standing; (2) friend of the court – amicus curia – status; and (3) informal intervention. Informal intervention is a catchall group that includes all the ways NGOs interact with international courts without being granted a formal procedure to do so. This section reviews some of the rules that regulate NGO intervention in several international courts.

1 *Standing*

Not everyone can be a party to a case before an international court. The ICJ is especially strict on this point, allowing only states to become parties.[1] While this rule obviously excludes NGOs, other international courts allow NGOs to acquire formal standing but only under certain conditions.

The ECHR allows NGOs to submit applications to it if they claim to be victims of a violation of the European Convention on Human Rights by a member state.[2] The victimhood requirement limits the ability of NGOs to litigate violations that infringe the rights of others, but do not have a direct impact on the NGO itself. NGOs committed to protecting vulnerable people that sometimes cannot apply themselves – for example because they are already dead – have challenged that rule with some success. The ECHR's *CLR* v. *Romania* judgment is revolutionary in this regard and will be discussed in Section 5.B.

The framers of other human rights courts have decided to deviate from the victimhood requirement and allow NGOs greater leeway to file applications. The African Court of Human Rights allows NGOs to serve as applicants even if they are not victims, but only if they were granted a special "observer status" and only vis-à-vis states that declared they are willing to accept cases initiated by such NGOs.[3] In the Inter-American human rights system, NGOs that are legally recognized in one or more of the members of the Organization of American States are allowed to file petitions with the American Commission on Human Rights even if they are not victims.[4] Notice that the commission screens petitions before they reach the IACHR itself.

[1] Statute of the International Court of Justice, Art. 34(1).

[2] European Convention on Human Rights, Art. 34.

[3] Protocol to the African Charter on Human and Peoples' Rights on the Establishment of the African Court on Human and Peoples' Rights, Art. 5(3), Art. 34(6).

[4] American Convention on Human Rights, Art. 44.

The conditions that limit the ability of NGOs to acquire standing show an ingrained suspicion against them. In the ECHR, a state is able to serve as applicant for violations in other European states that have nothing to do with it.[5] Unlike NGOs, States don't have to be victims to have standing. Nevertheless, very few cases over the court's history were initiated by states.[6] Perhaps the framers of the court rightly predicted that states are naturally restrained by the need to preserve political alliances, whereas NGOs and individuals do not have such restraints.

2 *Friends of the Court*

Amicus curiae briefs are a great way for an international court to receive valuable information and legal advice. In return for these benefits, NGOs that serve as friends of the court expect to influence judicial decisions. Many international courts preserve a substantial amount of discretion on which briefs they accept and which they choose to reject.

For example, the ECHR's President is granted the authority to invite anyone who is not an applicant to submit written comments or to take part in the court's hearings.[7] In 1982, the rules of the court first recognized the position of amicus curiae, although such interventions existed even before that date.[8] The rules of the court instruct the Chamber's President to allow interventions that are in the interest of the proper administration of justice and to let interveners participate in hearings in exceptional circumstances. Clearly, the rules give the President wide discretion. They even allow the President to set conditions for the intervention and to exclude the brief from the case file if these conditions are violated.[9]

The regulation of participation as friends of the court before the WTO AB is even less strictly defined. In fact, this court didn't have clear rules on the issue and had to shape the relevant rules by interpretation. In the *Shrimp Turtle* case, the Appellate Body decided to reject the Panel's

[5] European Convention on Human Rights, Art. 33.

[6] *See* Dragoljub Popovic, *Prevailing of Judicial Activism over Self-Restraint in the Jurisprudence of the European Court of Human Rights*, 42 CREIGHTON L. REV. 361, 372 (2009).

[7] European Convention on Human Rights, Art. 36(2).

[8] *See* LOVEDAY HODSON, NGOS AND THE STRUGGLE FOR HUMAN RIGHTS IN EUROPE 37–38 (2011).

[9] ECHR – Rules of Court, Rule 44(4).

interpretation and allow NGOs to submit briefs even if they were not formally requested to do so by the Panel.[10]

Theoretically, the ICJ is more stringent in limiting intervention by NGOs as friends of the court, but there are a couple of loopholes. The court may receive submissions from NGOs in advisory opinions proceedings.[11] In contentious cases, the ICJ is only allowed to formally receive information from international organizations of states.[12] Nevertheless, information from NGOs can reach the court if these organizations submit expert opinions or request one of the parties to annex this information to their own submission.[13]

3 *Informal Intervention*

A large part of the influence NGOs have on the decisions of international courts isn't regulated by formal court procedures. This is the realm of informal intervention. It includes everything from directly providing legal representation to applicants to giving the funds necessary for purchasing legal representation elsewhere. NGOs can even assist by simply offering advice and supplying information to potential applicants. This information can make all the difference between filing the case or not and may find the winning argument for someone with no former experience with the court's procedures.

For researchers, it is difficult to observe informal intervention because it may occur without leaving a trace in the court's official documents. Nevertheless, scholars have estimated that informal intervention in the ECHR accounts for much of the impact that NGOs have on this court.[14]

B When Should NGOs Participate?

Determining the optimal procedures for the intervention of NGOs before international courts is a complex exercise in cost-benefit analysis.

[10] WTO Appellate Body Report, United States – Import Prohibition of Certain Shrimp and Shrimp Products WT/DS58/AB/R (12 Oct. 1998) at par. 110.

[11] Statute of the International Court of Justice, Art. 66(2).

[12] Statute of the International Court of Justice, Art 34(2) allows the ICJ to receive information from "Public International Organizations." These are defined in art. 69(4) of the Rules of the Court as "international organizations of states" – clearly excluding NGOs.

[13] *See* Dinah Shelton, *The Participation of Nongovernmental Organizations in International Judicial Proceedings*, 88 AM. J. INT'L. L. 611, 628 (1994).

[14] *See* HODSON, Note 8 at 43–44, 56.

Furthermore, it would be naïve to assume that the same procedures should apply to all international courts. The best procedure depends on the relevant circumstances, and these are different from one court to the other.

The section addresses this problem in three stages: First, the advantages of NGO intervention are surveyed; then, the problems that arise from such intervention are analyzed; finally, different rules are suggested for different international courts.

1 *The Benefits of NGO Intervention*

International courts are created and funded to fulfill certain social goals.[15] NGO intervention is advantageous to the extent that it can help courts fulfill these goals without causing damage to other relevant interests. The help NGOs provide to international courts can be divided into three kinds: providing information and potential cases, improving the court's public relations, and assisting with the enforcement of the court's judgments. These are addressed in turn.

Inputs

Without cases, international courts cannot influence society. Therefore, NGOs who serve as applicants supply courts with the ultimate good – a possibility to decide cases. One can imagine that some courts – the ECHR being a prime example – actually have more cases than they can handle. But this doesn't imply that busy courts are harmed by NGO applications. In order to clean their dockets, international courts need mainly to solve the problem of repetitive cases that address essentially the same problem. The best way to do that is to produce one good judgment that would guide the court and the parties under its jurisdiction in all relevant future interactions.[16] To produce such a case, the court needs the right opportunity: a carefully selected set of circumstances that makes such a precedential ruling possible. NGOs have the expertise necessary to provide the court with such opportunities. Furthermore, as NGOs argue the

[15] *See* Shany, Note 12, Chapter 2 at 244–247.

[16] In fact, the ECHR creates specific avenues for such cases by using the Pilot Judgment procedure to require specific remedies from states to solve structural problems. More commonly, the Committee of Ministers incorporates this logic by monitoring compliance with so-called leading cases together with other cases that raise the same problem.

case, they would also uncover the legal reasoning that can be used by the court to support its judgment.

When NGOs serve as friends of the court, they do not directly bring the case, but they provide the court with information. This information includes legal arguments and relevant factual data that can help the court write a well-reasoned judgment. Furthermore, NGOs are also aware of the political landscape surrounding the case. In their briefs, or sometimes just by the willingness to put their name on such a brief, NGOs signal to the court the various political forces involved in the case. This can help the court make a decision that is politically wise and minimize the risk of backlash.

NGOs who help applicants informally provide them with legal reasons that eventually reach the court. In many cases, they render the application itself possible by making people aware of their rights and of the options they have to fight for them.

Public Relations

NGOs depend on publicity. In order to shape society according to their agenda, they need to be visible to the public. Usually, NGOs are funded by the public. To get more funds, they need more people to know about their activities. This gives NGOs a strong incentive to publish as much as possible their interaction with international courts. NGOs use their websites, their publications, as well as their connections with the traditional media to inform the public about the court proceedings in which they are involved. Every time an NGO disseminates information about its participation in a court case it is also doing the court a service – it is making the court known to more and more people. Usually, the NGO will try to present the court in the most favorable light because its image is very much connected to that of the court.

Sometimes, NGOs help the court's public relations in other ways. NGOs can fight for the court's interest against states that want to harm it. As an example, when European states convened the Brighton Conference and tried to limit the powers of the ECHR, NGOs issued a joint statement in support of the court and against its critics.[17] Because

[17] *See* Joint NGO Input to the Ongoing Negotiations on the Draft Brighton Declaration on the Future of the European Court of Human Rights, Mar. 20, 2012, available at: www.hrw.org/sites/default/files/related_material/2012_UK_Joint%20NGO%20input%20to%20the%20ongoing%20negotiations%20on%20the%20draft%20Brighton%20Declaration.pdf.

NGOs are so invested in the success of the court, they become its natural allies.

Enforcement

All international courts, whether compliance rates with their judgments are very high or very low, have to be aware that some of their judgments are not fully executed. Usually, international courts are limited in their ability to enforce their judgments, if they have enforcement powers at all. Courts must rely on reputational sanctions to encourage state compliance. But in order to shame states into compliance, information about their disobedience must be available to the international community. Courts simply do not have the resources to discover this information and to disseminate it.

NGOs are able to help international courts in these tasks. They can investigate the steps states actually take to comply with the courts' judgments and they can make this information publicly available. The best results are probably reached through collaboration of a formal institution – within or outside the court – with civil society. International courts are developing new mechanisms to facilitate such collaboration, one of which is described in Section 5.C.

The Reasons NGOs Are So Helpful

Now that the different ways NGOs contribute to international courts have been surveyed, it is possible to take a step back and explain more abstractly why NGOs can be so helpful. Counterintuitively, NGOs can help international courts be successful exactly because they are not formally committed to the success of these courts.

NGOs can choose whether to participate in international courts' proceedings or not. This implies that if NGOs decide in favor of participation, they send a powerful signal to the international community that they trust the court and believe in its ability to change state behavior. This signal can improve the court's reputation by suggesting to the international community that compliance with its judgments is expected.[18]

Furthermore, if some NGOs decide to stop collaborating with the court, they signal to the court that it needs to change its behavior to suit the interests of its interlocutors. This signal can help the court reform its

[18] *See* DOTHAN, Note 3, Chapter 1 at 3.

practices before it's too late. In this way, a well-informed pool of collaborators that are ready to commit such a form of "exit" can assist the court in routinely assessing its own behavior.[19]

To the extent that the court wants to prevent such exit by NGOs, it may be constrained to change the content of its judgments. But such a constraint is not always a liability. Sometimes, when an organization has to negotiate compromises against a strong adversary, it is beneficial to be constrained by a less pernicious third actor.[20] International courts are primarily worried about backlash from states. If courts can communicate to states that in some issues the courts' hands are tied since they are committed to the wishes of civil society, courts may gain greater leeway as a result.

2 *The Problems with NGO Intervention*

The first concern that may arise if NGOs are allowed to serve as applicants is exposing the court to cases it would rather not decide. Against this concern, it was argued that allowing NGO intervention doesn't necessarily mean opening the floodgates to numerous unnecessary cases. On the contrary, NGOs have the necessary expertise to select cases that are amenable for making doctrinal changes. These changes can solve structural problems that could potentially appear in many other repetitive cases. Furthermore, because NGOs are repeat players they have an interest in not tarnishing their professional reputation by bringing clearly inadequate cases.

A deeper problem with NGO intervention of any kind is that it may jeopardize the court's impartiality.[21] If NGOs take a stand in favor of one side of the dispute – whether they act as applicants, as friends of the court, or just aid this side informally – their large resources and their expertise may sway the result in favor of that side. This problem is particularly severe because NGOs, unlike individuals arguing their own case, may project an aura of objectivity that is often unmerited. The ability of NGOs to use their substantial influence while at the same time

[19] *See* HIRSCHMAN, Note 88, Chapter 2 at 24.

[20] *See* Robert D. Putnam, *Diplomacy and Domestic Politics: The Logic of Two-Level Games*, 42 INT'L ORG. 427, 440 (1988).

[21] *See* ERIC A. POSNER, THE PERILS OF GLOBAL LEGALISM 166–167 (2009) (suggesting that international courts are often biased because of the lack of proper mechanisms to ensure their impartiality); *see generally* Shai Dothan, Note 64, Chapter 3 (explaining how a bias of individual judges can translate to a bias of a court issuing judgments).

appearing to represent the public interest may bias the court's judgments. Furthermore, even if the court's judgments are not actually biased, people may fear that they are. The court could lose its image of evenhandedness and this would damage its legitimacy.

There is a larger issue here: Scholars have indicated that narrow interest groups can use international courts like the ECJ to shift the political balance of power in their own states.[22] NGOs can do exactly that. They can use litigation before international courts to make real policy changes in their countries. Some may approve of these changes in the name of liberal principles, but others may point out the loss of state sovereignty as well as the undermining of majoritarian decision-making by democratic bodies.

Allowing NGOs to intervene may often serve the interests of the weak and the indigent, but it is always important to remember that NGOs need money to survive. The rich and the powerful can use their resources to create or to buy-out NGOs that would do their bidding. There is even a catchy name for NGOs that submit to a certain government. These are known as GONGOs (Government-Organized Non-Governmental Organizations). Some may be rightly concerned that the relative strength of NGOs would simply recreate the relative wealth of the parties that support them. The wealthy would have more NGOs on their side.

This concern is real. Yet before making a decision on the procedures that allow NGO intervention one must ask: What is the alternative? Is it better to force the parties to file cases and briefs and to formulate legal arguments or would the poor fare better in the catch-as-catch-can competition of the open market? The legal arena isn't always just, but it is better than many other alternative arenas where powers compete. Dragging governments and powerful interest groups toward an arena where human rights and legal commitments mean something is often better than the alternative.

Another potential problem is that courts may rely on NGOs too much for legal research or for monitoring enforcement and lose the ability to fulfill these goals independently. This risk doesn't seem real at the moment, but international courts should constantly strive to preserve their competence to act even without the collaboration of NGOs. Too

[22] Karen J. Alter & Jeannette Vargas, *Explaining Variation in the Use of European Litigation Strategies: European Community Law and British Gender Equality Policy*, 33 Comp. Pol. Stud. 452, 453, 455–456, 473–474 (2000).

much reliance on an external organization may lead to undue influence. Alternatively, if the collaboration ends, the court may find itself helpless.

Finally, one may argue that NGOs waste valuable resources when they compete for greater influence over international courts. It is possible that money could be better spent on other things. Nevertheless, litigation before international courts may have positive side effects. Litigation draws attention to bad practices of states and recruits support for defending human rights and international law. These processes may lead to beneficial social changes over the long term, even if these changes are often unquantifiable.

3 *Setting Better Procedures for NGO Intervention*

It is clear from the analysis in the previous subsections that NGOs bring with them both advantages and disadvantages to international courts. The ultimate effect that NGOs will have depends on the relevant circumstances surrounding different courts. The impact also depends on the degree of involvement NGOs adopt: namely, do they serve as applicants, do they serve as friends of the court, or do they only intervene informally?

Generally speaking, the deeper the involvement of NGOs, the greater their willingness to contribute to the court. If NGOs are active as applicants, they are more likely to assist the public relations of the court and to help with the enforcement of judgments than if they are only friends of the court. NGOs who serve as friends of the court are generally more likely to contribute than NGOs who intervene informally.

There are several potential reasons for this phenomenon. First, if an NGO is deeply involved in a case, its reputation as an organization is tied to the success of the case. If an NGO acts as an applicant or even as a friend of the court, it wants to signal to its supporters that the court will find a violation and that this violation will be fully remedied. Second, when an NGO is involved in a case, it has to invest resources in acquainting itself with the facts and the relevant details. The NGO will also have to acquire specific expertise and to make professional connections in order to win the case. Once the judgment is issued, it is easy for the NGO to follow the case until compliance is secured because the principal investments have already been made.

Empirical research supports these hypotheses. The research described in Section 5.C included 137 ECHR judgments that drew NGO reports shaming states for noncompliance, which were published in an official website of the Committee of Ministers. Twenty-six of these judgments included amicus curiae briefs by NGOs. From these twenty-six judgments, fifteen included at least one report by an NGO who was previously involved as a friend of the court. When one considers that more than two hundred NGOs filed reports on the website, it is clear that NGOs are disproportionally more likely to follow through on cases in which they were involved as friends of the court. When NGO officials are asked about their tendency to follow through cases, some say that making sure cases are implemented is part of their strategy, others stress that they consider it their duty to ensure judgments they were involved in are complied with as much as possible, and some even say it is frowned upon in the NGO community to get involved in cases that were litigated by other NGOs without permission.[23]

The upshot of this analysis is that NGOs that are deeply involved can increase the benefits of the court. At the same time, the greater the degree of involvement, the more acute the problems raised by NGO intervention. In order to optimize the level of NGO intervention, it must be matched to the type of issues that specific international courts deal with.

Issues of war and peace such as the ones decided by the ICJ pose a special risk of politicization. Capture by NGOs may lead to severe damage to the court's objectivity and consequently to its legitimacy. It is therefore understandable that the ICJ prevents NGOs both from serving as applicants and from submitting amicus curiae briefs in contentious cases.[24]

The interests of the court also cannot be neglected. The IACHR is faced with many challenges, one of which is its very low compliance rate that some scholars assess as ranging between 5 and 12 percent.[25] More

[23] Shai Dothan, *A Virtual Wall of Shame: The New Way of Imposing Reputational Sanctions on Defiant States*, 27 Duke J. Comp. & Int'l. L. 141, 170 (2017).

[24] *See* Notes 1, 11–13.

[25] Eric A. Posner & John C. Yoo, *Judicial Independence in International Tribunals*, 93 Cal. L. Rev. 1, 43 (2005); Cavallaro & Brewer, Note 20, Chapter 4 at 786; Alexandra Huneeus, *Courts Resisting Courts: Lessons from the Inter-American Court's Struggle to Enforce Human Rights*, 44 Cornell Int'l. L. J. 493, 504 (2011). Compare Courtney Hillebrecht, Domestic Politics and International Human Rights Tribunals: The Problem of Compliance 44, 49, 51 (2014) (suggesting that focusing on compliance with specific obligations renders more positive compliance results); compare Øyvind Stiansen, *Competition and Compliance: Electoral Uncertainty and Implementation of Judgments from the International Human Rights Judiciary* 25 (draft available at https://papers.ssrn.com/sol3/papers.cfm?abstract_id=3116708) (presenting different compliance results conditioned on the degree of national political competition).

and more, this court is forced to perceive itself primarily as a theater for contestation and for the dissemination of information.[26] For that, the court needs as much publicity as it can get. This means that NGOs are essential for the court's effectiveness and may justify the fact that NGOs can file petitions with the Inter-American Commission on Human Rights, which refers cases to the IACHR, even if the NGOs themselves were not victims of any violation, as long as they are recognized by one of the states in the Organization of American States.[27] The challenges faced by the court may also explain the fact that it has never refused to accept an amicus curiae brief and that such briefs are received in about a third of its cases.[28]

The advantages and disadvantages of NGOs' participation in international courts' proceedings must always be assessed in light of other plausible alternatives. It is true that international litigation is an arena where the rich and powerful may often come out ahead, a fact often highlighted by critics of the WTO AB. This is why when this court allowed the submission of briefs by NGOs even without a formal request by a panel in the *Shrimp Turtle case*,[29] critics in developing states voiced concerns that the NGOs that will influence the court were captured by richer countries.[30]

Nevertheless, the rich have an advantage in almost every arena where powers compete. Often the law and the legal discourse can act as equalizers and lead to more just outcomes than any alternative arena of contestation. Therefore, courts like the WTO AB that deal with states with starkly different levels of wealth are expected to draw criticism from both rich and poor countries if they choose to allow NGO participation. It is difficult to recommend an optimal rule for courts of this kind.

Sometimes, however, international courts can be relatively certain that NGO intervention is beneficial and could be facilitated by making small changes without unpredictable harmful consequences. The ECHR case of *CLR* v. *Romania* is a good example.[31]

[26] *See* Cavallaro & Brewer, Note 20, Chapter 4 at 792–795.

[27] *See* Note 4.

[28] *See* Yaël Ronen & Yael Naggan, *Third Parties, in* THE OXFORD HANDBOOK OF INTERNATIONAL ADJUDICATION 806 at p. 824 (Cesare Romano, Karen Alter, & Yuval Shany, eds., 2013).

[29] *See* Note 10.

[30] *See* Peter Van den Bossche, *NGO Involvement in the WTO: A Comparative Perspective*, 11 J. INT'L. ECON. L. 717, 721 (2008).

[31] CLR v. Romania, judgment of July 17, 2014, Reports of Judgments and Decisions EUR. Ct. H.R. 2014.

The tragic case concerned the death of Valentin Câmpeanu, a Roma child who was ill with HIV-AIDS and also suffered from severe intellectual disability. The child was hospitalized in the Poina Mare Neuropsychiatric hospital in Romania. On the day of his death at the age of eighteen, he was visited by a representative of the Centre for Legal Resources (CLR) – a Romanian based NGO. CLR reported that Valentin was closed up in an isolated room and ignored by the staff, who were afraid of being infected by his illness. Clearly, he didn't receive appropriate treatment. Furthermore, other patients were also mistreated and many had previously died in the same hospital.

The CLR tried to initiate domestic proceedings against those accountable for the boy's death. When these proceedings failed, the CLR filed an application to the ECHR claiming that Romania violated the deceased's right to life and other rights. The ECHR explained in its judgment that none of the traditional categories that make cases admissible apply in this case. Without changing the rules of admissibility, the ECHR could not hear the case.[32]

In order not to contradict the spirit of the European Convention on Human Rights by allowing Romania to escape from responsibility for the boy's death, the court decided to change the rules of admissibility. It allowed CLR to act as the representative of the deceased even though the organization wasn't accepted as the boy's attorney and the application was lodged after his death. CLR was not a victim of a violation itself and therefore would be denied standing by the court's traditional rules. The judgment is a clear example of bending the rules of admissibility to fulfill higher values enshrined in the Convention. However, the consequences of such expansive interpretation are easily contained – they are not expected to harm anyone and may do justice with those who cannot fight for their rights.

The ECHR kept a wide discretion on which NGOs will be allowed standing in "exceptional circumstances."[33] Judge Pinto De Albuquerque wrote a concurring opinion in which he supported setting a clear test instead: non-victims would have standing when the victims are especially vulnerable and do not have relatives, guardians, or legal representatives.[34]

[32] *Id*, at par. 105.

[33] *Id*, at par. 112.

[34] Judge Pinto De Albuquerque's concurring opinion at par. 11. It is important to note in this regard that according to the ECHR's prior judgments, relatives of deceased victims can serve as applicants if they claim a violation of the victim's right to life. *See* Fairfield and Others v. The United Kingdom, 08.03.2005 Reports of Judgments and Decisions ECtHR 2005-VI.

The majority's judgment provides less guidance to future applicants, but allows the court to make the decision on admissibility based on the specific circumstances of each case, limiting the possibility of harmful repercussions. The court could consider of course the vulnerability of the victims and their inability to bring cases themselves or through relatives and legal representative, but it could also consider the suitability of the NGO to represent the rights of the victims and the need to decide the case to serve public policy.

NGO participation can be improved even without changing the rules of admissibility as the court did in *CLR* v. *Romania*. Scholars have noted that sometimes NGOs do not participate for reasons that are practical and not doctrinal. NGOs may not know enough about the procedures of the court and may not be aware of pending cases where they could contribute by filing amicus curiae briefs. NGOs may decide against filing such briefs because they feel their intervention isn't sufficiently mentioned in the court's judgments to make it worth their effort.[35] If that is the case, NGOs can be encouraged to intervene by disseminating more information about ongoing cases, making the conditions for intervention clear and public, and mentioning the contributions of NGOs in the court's judgments and publications.

Informal NGO intervention cannot be directly regulated by court procedures, but this doesn't mean that the policies of the court cannot influence it. If legal fees are regularly reimbursed by the court, this can increase the incentive of poorly funded NGOs to represent more applicants. If the court invests in publicizing its judgments, this can improve the chances that NGOs who seek publicity will get involved in more cases.

C International Courts Provide Arenas for Fruitful NGO Deliberation

At the end of a long process, an international court has issued a final judgment. The work of the judges is now done and so is the race to influence their decision. The social impact of the judgment, however, is yet to be determined. Because international courts usually do not have effective sanctions against states that fail to comply with their judgments, states can be persuaded to comply mainly by the force of

[35] Hodson, Note 8 at 52–55 (explaining why there are too few NGOs serving as friends of the court in the ECHR).

reputational sanctions. NGOs play a vital role in this regard. They can expose noncompliance by states and shame them into changing their behavior.

The process of shaming that NGOs engage in raises a potential problem: are the reports against the states' practices true or false? Rumors that travel between a large group of people – many of them biased or motivated by personal interest – can easily spiral out of control. At the same time, if lawyers and activists know one another and are aware of each other's biases, they may be able to screen out bad information and collectively reach truthful impressions.

These are empirical hypotheses about the way information passes through social networks. The first, pessimistic hypothesis is known as the "echo" hypothesis. The second is known as the "bandwidth" hypothesis.[36] Both have theoretical justifications, which are discussed later on in this chapter. But the only way to determine whether the work of NGOs who follow up on international judgments fits the echo hypothesis or the bandwidth hypothesis is through empirical investigation.

This section provides such an investigation. It tracks reputational sanctions used by NGOs against states that failed to comply with judgments of the ECHR. The research is focused on a new website launched by the Committee of Ministers of the Council of Europe (CM) in 2011. On the website, reports by NGOs accusing states of noncompliance with ECHR judgments are published, together with responses that states choose to offer to such accusations. All the reports published in the first four years of the website's existence were coded, together with the judgments they addressed. This quantitative study – complemented by interviews with lawyers and activists in NGOs that published reports – can throw light on the way information moves through numerous NGOs and determine whether civil society complies with the echo hypothesis or the bandwidth hypothesis.[37]

1 The Case Study

The ECHR issues many hundreds of judgments every year, yet its ability to enforce these judgments is severely limited. The body in charge of

[36] *See* Ronald S. Burt, Brokerage and Closure: An Introduction to Social Capital 167–168 (2005).

[37] *See generally* Dothan, Note 23.

enforcing ECHR judgments is the CM, which monitors compliance using the Department of Execution of Judgments (DEJ). Theoretically, the CM can expel a state from the Council of Europe for noncompliance with ECHR judgments.[38] However, this extreme measure was never used in the past, and its future use seems close to impossible.[39] The ECHR and the CM must rely primarily on reputational sanctions in order to convince states to comply.

The CM has developed a series of procedures that aid it in shaming states into compliance. No more than six months after a judgment becomes final, the state is required to submit a so-called action report, which should describe the measures taken by the state to comply and a timeline for taking further necessary measures. If the state fails to comply on time, the CM will discuss the state's actions and require it to change its behavior. If the state continues not to comply, the CM may issue an open criticism of the state known as an "interim resolution."[40]

To streamline the process of enforcement, the CM divides cases into two tracks: standard procedure and enhanced procedure. Cases in the enhanced procedure involve persistent noncompliance, and they are more regularly discussed in the CM's meetings. Acknowledging that many cases reflect widespread problems that appear in numerous other cases, the CM started to group cases dealing with the same problem behind a "leading case." The CM monitors compliance with the leading case together with all the other cases that raise the same violation.

In 2011, the new website of the DEJ was launched. On this website, the DEJ publishes all the action reports produced by states and the interim resolutions issued against states. According to rule 9.2 of the CM rules, the CM can consider communications from NGOs and national human rights institutions. In an effort to disclose more information about the actual compliance of states, these communications are also published on the website. Once the CM receives a report by an NGO criticizing a state for noncompliance with a judgment, it sends the report to the state, which then has the option to respond within five days. After five days, the

[38] *See* Statute of the Council of Europe, Art. 8.

[39] Despite the fact that no state was formally expelled, threats of expulsion eventually led Greece to leave the Council of Europe in 1969.

[40] *See* Lucja Miara & Victoria Prais, *The Role of Civil Society in the Execution of Judgments of the European Court of Human Rights*, 5 Eur. Hum. Rt. L. Rev. 528, 531 (2012).

report is published on the website, together with any response the state chose to issue.

From the launching of the website until December 2014, 266 NGO reports were published. The reports addressed 137 ECHR judgments. Reports were filed by over two hundred NGOs, many of them very small and specialized. Sometimes, several NGOs participated in filing the same report or filed separate reports about the same judgment.

2 *The Focus on Issues That Matter*

How is it possible to test whether information that flows through the NGO community becomes better or worse? One solution is to study the issues that NGOs focus on. If NGOs focus on severe violations and on legally important issues, then they collectively process information in a good way. If the network focuses on the issues that matter – that infringe vital human rights or pertain to fundamental legal problems – then NGOs improve the information that passes between them instead of corrupting it.

To check if that is indeed the case, the paper makes two sets of comparisons. The first comparison contrasts all the 137 cases that were subject to one or more NGO reports to a much larger group of cases from around the same time that did not lead to an NGO report. The second group, which can be called the "general population of cases" includes all the Chamber and Grand Chamber judgments issued in English from January 1, 2008 to October 31, 2013 in which the ECHR found at least one violation and which did not lead to an NGO report. This general population includes 5,584 judgments. If the cases that led to NGO reports are, on average, different from cases that didn't lead to a NGO report, this suggests that NGOs focus on issues of a certain kind.

The second comparison also tries to establish where NGOs spend the most resources. It divides cases that led to NGO reports according to the amount of attention dedicated to them by the NGO community. Attention is measured by three proxies: the number of reports per case, the number of NGOs involved in all these reports, and the total number of pages in all these reports. The study compared fifty-four cases with "minimal" NGO attention – only one report, filed by one NGO, which holds no more than ten pages – against thirty-eight cases with "special" NGO attention – two reports or more, filed by two or more NGOs, which hold at least eleven pages. If cases with special NGO attention are different from cases with minimal NGO attention, the network of NGOs probably focuses on the type of cases that resemble those in the special attention group.

The first step in testing whether NGOs focus on cases with severe human rights violations is dividing cases according to the type of right that was infringed. The Convention that the ECHR is tasked with applying contains a variety of rights. Some rights such as the right to life and the right against torture, protected in Articles 2 and 3 of the Convention, are meant to protect against serious and severe violations. Other rights, such as the right to a fair trial protected by Article 6, usually protect against violations that are less severe. While the type of right infringed doesn't describe the magnitude of the violation – violations of fundamental rights can be limited in their effect while violations of more mundane rights can harm people significantly – the article that was violated is a useful proxy for the severity of the violation.

An analysis of the types of violations involved in cases in the general population and in the group of cases that led to NGO reports reveals statistically significant differences. There are a significantly greater proportion of Article 2 and Article 3 violations in cases that led to NGO reports. These articles deal with such severe violations that states cannot derogate from them even in times of emergency. The focus of NGOs on cases of this kind suggests that NGOs concentrate on severe violations, which implies that they collectively process information well.

Another significant difference between the articles violated in the general population and in cases that led to NGO reports concerns Articles 13 and 14 of the Convention. Article 13 protects against failing to supply victims with an effective remedy for another violation. Article 14 requires states not to discriminate in their protection of Convention rights. Naturally, applicants often accuse states of violating these two articles in addition to other Convention articles. After all, most persistent human rights violations are not properly remedied and involve some measure of discrimination. But the ECHR usually decides that finding a violation of these two articles is redundant when a violation of a specific right is found. Only in unique cases of a continuous abuse of rights or discriminatory practices would the ECHR find a violation of Articles 13 and 14. The data shows that there are proportionally more violations of these two articles in cases that led to an NGO report, compared to the general population. This indicates a focus by NGOs on severe and extensive human rights violations.

A comparison of cases that led to minimal NGO attention with cases that led to special NGO attention doesn't render significant results regarding some of the articles examined in this section. Nevertheless, cases with special NGO attention have a significantly greater proportion of Article 14 violations. This suggests that even when NGOs are involved, they would invest greater resources in cases of widespread discrimination.

A focus on severe violations is one indicator that NGOs target the issues that matter. But a severe violation doesn't necessarily equal a legally important case. Unfortunately, states can do horrible things to their citizens without any legal novelty. In contrast, mild human rights violations can lead to cases of great legal significance. A clear example is the famous *Von Hannover* case[41] – known for its innovative balance between privacy and freedom of the press – which concerned the permissibility of publishing paparazzi pictures of the princess of Monaco. To firmly establish that NGOs focus on valuable cases, the relative legal importance of cases that draw their attention must be examined.

The best proxy for the legal importance of cases is actually the categorization of cases by the ECHR HUDOC database. All cases in the database are divided according to their importance into four different levels: Case Reports, and importance levels 1, 2, and 3. Case Reports cases are selected for official publication and they are the cases with the greatest legal significance. Level 1 cases are not officially published, but they still contribute significantly to the development, modification, or clarification of the ECHR's judgments. Level 2 cases do not make a significant contribution to the court's case law, but they are a little more than just applying existing law, while Level 3 cases only apply preexisting law without changing it.[42]

Cases that led to NGO reports are significantly more likely to be categorized as either Case Reports or Level 1 cases. In fact, while most of the cases in the general population are Level 3 cases, more than half of the cases that led to NGO reports are Case Reports or Level 1 cases. Furthermore, cases that led to special NGO attention are significantly more likely to be categorized as Case Reports or Level 1 cases than cases with only minimal NGO attention. These data suggest that NGOs do focus primarily on cases of legal importance.

[41] Von Hannover v. Germany, 2004-III Eur. Ct. H.R. 1.

[42] *See* ECHR HUDOC User Manual 11–12 (2012), available at www.echr.coe.int/Documents/HUDOC_Manual_2012_ENG.pdf.

Another method of assessing legal importance is checking if the cases were assigned to a Chamber or to a Grand Chamber. Chambers are panels of seven judges, while Grand Chamber cases are decided by seventeen judges – a panel used only in cases of extreme legal importance.[43] In the general population less than 1 percent of the cases were Grand Chamber Judgments, while cases that led to an NGO report included about 15 percent of Grand Chamber judgments: a large and statistically significant difference. There is also a significantly greater proportion of Grand Chamber cases in cases that led to special NGO attention compared to cases that led to minimal NGO attention.

The study also reveals that NGOs focus their attention on cases that involve dissents or concurring opinions. There are proportionally more cases with separate opinions in the group of cases that led to NGO reports compared to the general population. There are also more judgments with separate opinions in cases with special NGO attention compared to cases with minimal NGO attention. These differences are statistically significant. They reveal that NGOs focus on cases that are important enough in the eyes of the judges to incentivize them to write a separate opinion.

To conclude, the data clearly show that NGOs concentrate on cases that are both legally important and involve severe human rights violations. This is what you would expect to see if information flowing through the elaborate NGO community becomes better, not worse. But before explaining why NGOs live in a "bandwidth" world – a network that improves the assessments of its members – another aspect of the issues NGOs focus on must be examined.

3 *The Focus on Well-Behaving States*

Did you ever wonder which countries suffer the most from shaming by the international community? States like Russia try to convince the world

[43] A case can be referred to a Grand Chamber by the Chamber, if the judges in the Chamber find that the case raises a serious question of interpretation or if the case might lead to a digression from prior judgments. Alternatively, after the Chamber issues a judgment and before this judgment becomes final, a party to the case can ask that it be referred to the Grand Chamber. This referral will only be granted if the case raises a significant issue of interpretation or an issue of great importance. See Articles 30–31, 42–44 to the Convention.

that they are the target of accusations only because they are considered to be the "black sheep" of Europe. In contrast, states like the United Kingdom would argue that they face a larger share of accusations because their relatively good human rights practices lead to especially high expectations by civil society. The case study described in this section can help determine which side of the debate is right. In the process, valuable lessons can be learned about the way reputational sanctions are used by the network of NGOs.

The first step in this enquiry involves deciding which are the low-reputation states – states that routinely disobey international law – and which are the high-reputation states. To avoid prejudiced judgments, the paper created a metric based entirely on quantitative data about state behavior vis-à-vis the ECHR and the CM. States obtained scores based on factors such as the number of pending cases before the ECHR, the number of ECHR judgments that found a violation, and the number of cases awaiting compliance before the CM. Eventually, the metric exposes states such as Russia, Poland, Turkey, and Romania as low-reputation states. In contrast, states like France, Germany, Spain, and the United Kingdom are classified as high-reputation states.

When the proportions of cases that led to NGO reports and cases in the general population are measured for the groups of all low-reputation states and all high-reputation states, a significant difference emerges. High-reputation states are significantly more likely to generate cases that lead to NGO reports. This may suggest that NGOs deliberately target their shaming efforts against states that are usually well-behaving.

Several possible reasons come to mind as potential explanations for this pattern. The paper checks whether high-reputation states are more likely to respond to NGOs' accusations, giving them an incentive to file more reports. It finds no significant difference in responsive behavior between the two types of states. No significant difference is found also in the propensity of the two types of states to file action reports: plans on how to comply with a judgment that could give NGOs necessary information. As far as compliance with the specific judgment in question – leading to closing the case by the CM until January 2015 – is concerned, there is also no significant difference between the two types of states.

One may think that NGOs are more common in high-reputation states and find it easier to work there. If NGOs start to get involved in cases that are being litigated, they may feel committed to monitor compliance with them later on. However, there is no significant difference between the past involvement of NGOs as friends of the court in the cases that led to reports regarding the two types of states. Other forms of past involvement, such as by funding legal assistance or providing advice, are much more difficult to track.

Although high-reputation states usually draw cases of greater legal importance than low-reputation states, this difference cannot explain the focus of NGOs on high-reputation states because cases that led to NGO reports do not differ significantly in their importance levels between the two types of states.

After alternative explanations have been excluded, the evidence seems to support the hypothesis that NGOs do concentrate their attention on high-reputation states. But why do they do that? A series of interviews with NGO activists and lawyers, including from organizations who filed reports that appear on the database, seems to suggest that the reason behind this pattern is strategic.

NGO activists stressed repeatedly that they are committed to social change. While they have to compete with other organizations for limited funds, their ultimate goal is to make states improve their practices. This is why they often cooperate with other organizations and try to work together to reach their goals.

The key difference between high-reputation states and low-reputation states is in how they respond to activism by NGOs. In high-reputation states, the government is willing to listen to criticism and to try to improve its practices. Moreover, local officials respect the work of NGOs, learn from them, and even communicate with them directly. Resources spent on high-reputation states can lead to real results, because the general atmosphere is receptive to the work of NGOs. Activists stressed that they would not turn a blind eye to violations just because they are committed by a country that is usually well-behaving. Instead, a country that is willing to improve provides an opportunity to fix what went wrong.

In low-reputation states, the situation is very different. Countries like Russia and Romania seem not to care at all about the reports filed against them. NGOs that focus on these countries are using the Committee of Ministers to try to pressure their governments, but they cannot hope to get direct answers from officials in their own countries. Furthermore, NGOs operating in low-reputation states are often subject to continuous bureaucratic harassment by their government and a very hostile public sentiment.[44]

In light of that, it can be concluded that NGOs believe high-reputation states care more about their international reputation than low-reputation states. This is why high-reputation states are more susceptible to shaming and are likely to improve their behavior when they are subjected to reputational sanctions. Low-reputation states, in contrast, simply don't care enough about their reputation to change their behavior when they are subjected to criticism. NGOs make a rational decision not to waste their time on shaming low-reputation states.

This finding lends further support to the possibility that information flowing through NGO networks gets better over time. NGOs seem to focus their resources on high-reputation states because they expect high-reputation states to care more about their reputation than low-reputation states. This concurs with the common theoretical analysis of reputation, which suggests that high-reputation states generally value their reputation more than low-reputation states. Scholars have argued for years that a high-reputation state loses more from a similar reputational sanction than a low-reputation state. The explanation provided by these scholars is purely theoretical: misconduct by high-reputation states cuts against strong prior expectations of the international community and therefore requires a more radical updating of these expectations than similar misconduct by a low-reputation state.[45] Finding that NGOs focus most of their energy on criticizing states that care about this criticism naturally suggests that NGOs base their actions on good information. The network seems to have a beneficial effect on the information available to its members.

4 *Why NGOs Form a Bandwidth World*

In a bandwidth world, information that travels through the network becomes more accurate over time. That is, unmerited accusations are refuted while true accusations are repeated. Every member of the network knows enough about the biases of others to distinguish between

[44] *See* Dothan, Note 23 at 175–179.

[45] *See* Oona A. Hathaway, *Between Power and Principle: An Integrated Theory of International Law*, 72 U. Chi. L. Rev. 469, 510 (2005); Guzman, Note 33, Chapter 3 at 83; Dothan, Note 3, Chapter 1 at 13.

true and false statements. In contrast, in an echo world biases pile up as every member of the network adds his own prejudiced misconception of events. Members feel a need to conform to the group even when it is misguided and their close connections to other members make them too credulous of others' opinions. The result is a quick corruption of information and multiplying falsehoods.[46] The empirical evidence presented in this section suggests that NGOs who monitor compliance with judgments of international courts tend to form a bandwidth world. Why is that?

Theoretical and empirical research in Social Network Analysis and related fields can provide some answers. Based on this research, it seems that the first quality which makes the network of NGOs so effective at processing information is the relative independence of NGOs from one another. While NGOs often collaborate and they certainly learn from each other, they do not have to surrender to pressures from other NGOs. The independence of NGOs prevents them from cascading after the opinion of others without checking the facts.

The common model used to explain the problem of succumbing to peer-pressure is known as a "threshold model." A threshold describes the number of accusations by other members of the network that a member would have to hear before inevitably repeating the accusation. If NGOs were dependent on each other, the number of accusations they would have to hear before joining the crowd would be small. They would have a "low threshold" – a dangerous recipe for producing false rumors.[47] But fortunately, NGOs have a high threshold. Their independence means they are not constrained to follow the group, allowing them to prevent lies and exaggerations from spreading.

The theoretical insights about the tendency of cohesive groups to propagate misrepresentation of events are supported by empirical research on group deliberation. In groups that contain individuals with strong social ties to each other, discussion leads to more extreme views. When social ties are strong, the price of going against the current may be unbearable.[48] NGOs are saved from this predicament exactly because the ties between them are quite loose.

[46] *See* Burt, Note 36 at 167–168.

[47] *See* Mark Granovetter, *Threshold Models of Collective Behavior*, 83 Amer. J. Soc. 1420, 1423, 1429 (1978).

[48] *See* Cass R. Sunstein, *Deliberative Trouble? Why Groups Go to Extremes*, 110 Yale L. J. 71, 90–92 (2000).

Another fact that protects NGOs from forming an echo world is the large differences between them. If members of a group are similar, they are likely to have similar views and the result is that every member of the group is exposed to a limited set of arguments. Groups that share a small and skewed pool of arguments are easily pushed to extremes.[49] NGOs are immune from this problem because they are so diverse. Some NGOs are very big and some are very small. The staff at the NGOs in the database comes from a variety of countries and cultural backgrounds. These activists and lawyers possess a plethora of contrasting ideologies that protect them from herd behavior.

Finally, NGOs have another characteristic that was proven by the experimental literature to prevent cascades of views: They have narrowly defined roles. Each NGO has a specific agenda that it is committed to, a public agenda. Experiments have shown that actors with specific roles that are known to the rest of the group stop the corruption of information that accompanies some group deliberations.[50]

Because of these reasons, the network of NGOs tends to improve the quality of information that flows in it about human rights violations by states. The European Convention on Human Rights, however, showed only limited trust in NGOs – allowing them to serve as applicants only when they are themselves a victim of a violation, at least until *CLR* v. *Romania* changed that. In contrast, the Convention assumed that other states are the best protectors of human rights and allowed every member state to bring a case against another state even if the violation doesn't concern the applicant state in any way. Unless the framers of the Convention intended to minimize the number of applications, their bet was probably misguided: States brought very few cases to the ECHR and a large portion of these cases were clearly political pay-backs.[51]

States lack the qualities that make the network of NGOs into a bandwidth world. They are connected in a dense web of alliances that makes it very difficult for them to step out of line. States cannot afford to have one distinct agenda. They are always forced to balance numerous

[49] *See id*, at 89–90.

[50] Cass. R. Sunstein & Reid Hastie, Wiser: Getting Beyond Groupthink to Make Groups Smarter 111–112 (2015).

[51] *See* Scott Leckie, *The Inter-State Complaint Procedure in International Human Rights Law: Hopeful Prospects or Wishful Thinking?* 10 Hum. Rts Q. 249, 254 (1988).

political interests at the same time. This is why states are pressured not to accuse other states or, more rarely, to repeat false accusations because of political interests.

There is, however, one advantage that states have over NGOs: States are usually accountable for their accusations. In contrast, NGOs are relatively cheap to create and can hide the real powers behind their actions. NGOs, or the so-called GONGOs, could be used by states and other interest groups to smear the reputation of other states with impunity. Nevertheless, the transparency of the website discussed in this study allows everyone to see the reports filed by NGOs and to assess the evidence they are based on. This limits the danger posed by the ability of easily constructed NGOs to mask the true interests that motivate their accusations.

D Conclusion

The cooperation between international courts and NGOs can be mutually beneficial. NGOs provide courts with cases to decide, public exposure, and assistance in enforcing their judgments. Courts give NGOs a chance to shape the law and to spread their message. But this partnership could be harmful if it is not properly regulated. This is why good procedures for NGO participation are essential.

NGOs can make another important contribution: They can improve and magnify the reputational sanctions waged against non-compliant states. Despite the empirical findings which suggest that – in some settings – NGO involvement makes the information about states' actual behavior more accurate, the official court system cannot relax its guard. The CM, for example, may be called upon to issue a final statement about state compliance with the ECHR's judgments. It is crucial that this statement is believed and accepted by the international community.

Part of the reason courts are needed is to give states that committed violations a way to repair their mistakes and regain their reputation.[52] A clear stipulation of what a state has to do to amend its ways or a

[52] *See* Lisa Bernstein, *Opting Out of The Legal System: Extralegal Contractual Relations in the Diamond Industry*, 21 J. LEGAL STUD. 115, 126 (1992) (highlighting that when the community agrees on a certain penalty, this helps repair the reputation damaged by the initial misconduct).

pronouncement that the state fully complied with its obligations can stop the cycle of accusations against a state that has strayed but redeemed itself. An objective and legitimate international court is essential not only for making a formal accusation against states. It also gives states a way to atone for their misbehavior.

6

Creating the Right Incentives

The easiest way to think of the problem of intervention by international courts is to juxtapose an international court and a state. If there is reason to believe that the state can make a better decision than the court, then the court should defer to the state and respect the principle of subsidiarity. If, in contrast, there is reason to believe that the court can make a better decision, it should be allowed to intervene.

This simplistic picture may work some of the time. But sometimes it overlooks dynamics within the state that could fundamentally change the ultimate outcome of international courts' intervention. A good example for a case in which considering only the dyad court-state could result in error is the rule of complementarity that regulates the intervention of the ICC.

Complementarity is a rule of admissibility that prevents the ICC from accepting cases that were prosecuted or investigated at the state level. Scholars noted the apparent similarity between complementarity and other rules that reflect the overarching principle of subsidiarity, such as the margin of appreciation.[1] What these rules have in common is that they circumscribe the ability of international courts to intervene in domestic affairs and regulate the division of labor between international courts and domestic bodies. But the rule of complementarity is different from other rules of judicial deference, because the purpose of the ICC is different than that of other international courts.

One major goal of the ICC is to deter international crimes.[2] This means that the ICC attempts to directly incentivize soldiers not to commit crimes. The principle of complementarity implies that the ICC

[1] *See* Simon Hentrei, *Generalising the Principle of Complementarity: Framing International Judicial Authority*, 4 Trans. Leg. Theo. 419, 435 (2013).

[2] *See* The International Court: Challenges to Achieving Justice and Accountability in the 21st Century 13 (Mark S. Ellis & Richard J. Goldstone, eds., 2008).

cannot touch soldiers that were prosecuted domestically. This has a direct effect on their incentives. At the same time, the promise of non-intervention by the ICC in case of a genuine national prosecution gives states an incentive to prosecute soldiers themselves. This also affects the incentives of soldiers within the state and may deter them from committing crimes. The dyad court-state becomes a triad court-state-soldier. The intervention of international courts doesn't just add on to domestic mechanisms of justice.[3] It changes the behavior of national bodies as well as the behavior of individual soldiers. Without understanding this dynamic, one cannot assess the deterrent effect of the ICC.

This chapter suggests that the rule that regulates intervention by international criminal courts – complementarity or the more limiting rule of primacy – could shape the deterrence of international crimes. Moreover, the chapter suggests that the appropriate rule doesn't only depend on the quality of the judiciary within states. It also depends on the probability of prosecution by the ICC. A rise in the probability of prosecution can change the recommended rule from the current rule of complementarity to the rule of primacy favored by the ad-hoc criminal tribunals in Rwanda and the former Yugoslavia.

The analysis is pushed yet another step backward to address the effect of the rule of admissibility on the willingness of states to join the ICC's jurisdiction. This has interesting parallels with other rules on intervention by international courts. Such rules may determine the type of countries that are actually subject to the judgments of an international court.

A The ICC and Potential Rules of Admissibility

In 2002, the first permanent international criminal court in history was created – the ICC. This court is tasked with prosecuting the most severe international crimes, including genocide, crimes against humanity, and war crimes. Many had great hopes for the ICC, and more than 120 countries agreed to join its jurisdiction. More than sixteen years after the

[3] ICC intervention isn't just another sieve that can deter more soldiers who are not deterred domestically. Rather, ICC intervention changes deterrence at the domestic level as well. Compare Jakob von Holderstein Holtermann, *A "Slice of Cheese" – A Deterrence-Based Argument for the International Criminal Court*, 11 Hum. Rts. Rev. 289, 303–304 (2010) (making the contrary argument that the ICC is only adding another layer of deterrence or "slice of Swiss cheese").

inception of the court, however, its critics are multiplying. Critics point to the court's incredibly slow proceedings and ask if the conviction of two – rather unimportant – international criminals in the court's first twelve years justifies paying over a billion dollars in costs.[4] Some doubt the feasibility of deterring soldiers accustomed to living by the sword,[5] and others are outraged by the court's almost exclusive focus on Africa.[6]

This grim picture doesn't mean that the ICC has no future. Many international courts – the best example is probably the ECHR – had humble beginnings and developed quite nicely. Actual deterrence of international crimes by the ICC may look like a dream for now, but may become reality tomorrow.

The ICC adopted the rule of complementarity according to which it is unable to prosecute a soldier if (1) that soldier is being investigated or prosecuted legitimately by a state, (2) the state has already decided not to prosecute that soldier after a legitimate investigation,[7] or (3) a national court decided the case legitimately.[8]

Complementarity is different from the rule of primacy, which was adopted by the International Criminal Tribunal for the former Yugoslavia (ICTY) and the International Criminal Tribunal for Rwanda (ICTR). These courts are preempted from taking a case only if the accused was subject to a full and legitimate trial for an international crime.[9] As long as a person is being investigated, prosecuted, and tried, the ad-hoc tribunals can request the state to defer to their own jurisdiction.[10]

[4] *See* David Davenport, *International Criminal Court: 12 years, $1 Billion, 2 Convictions*, Forbes Mar. 12, 2014.

[5] Julian Ku & Jide Nzelibe, *Do International Criminal Tribunals Deter or Exacerbate Humanitarian Atrocities*, 84 Wash. U. L. Rev. 777, 783 (2006).

[6] *See* the discussion at https://iccforum.com/africa.

[7] Rome Statute of the International Criminal Court July 17, 1998, 2187 U.N.TS. 90 (Rome Statute), art. 17(1) (a–b).

[8] Rome Statute, art. 17(1)(c), art. 20(3)

[9] *See* Updated Statute of the International Criminal Tribunal for the Former Yugoslavia (Sep. 2009) (ICTY Statute), art. 10(2). Statute of the International Criminal Tribunal for Rwanda (November 1994) (ICTR Statute), art. 9(2). The requirement that the trial will be for an international crime, as opposed to an ordinary crime, is another obstacle that makes it harder to preempt the ad-hoc tribunals from intervening compared to the ICC. *See* Kevin Jon Heller, *A Sentence-Based Theory of Complementarity*, 53 Harv. Int'l L.J. 85, 93 (2012). International trials require specific legislation and are more difficult to prove, *see* id at 94–95, 100–103.

[10] *See* ICTY Statute, art. 9, ICTR Statute, art. 8.

B The Rule that Maximizes Deterrence

Which rule leads to better deterrence, complementarity or primacy? The answer depends on the circumstances facing the ICC. The analysis in this section proceeds under the reasonable assumption that the ICC cannot expose sham trials at the national level. The ICC may be prevented from exposing fraudulent proceedings either because it lacks information or because it fears the political backlash that would result from presenting the state as a cheat. Section 6.C explains how the analysis changes if sham trials can be exposed, at least under certain conditions.

The discussion about the deterrence of soldiers starts with the assumption that soldiers make a rational decision when they choose to commit or not to commit crimes. Soldiers may have an incentive to commit war crimes such as willful killing, torture, or taking of hostages in order to increase their chances of fulfilling their military objectives. Sometimes, such war crimes are also used by soldiers to reduce the risk to themselves or their subordinates. Soldiers will balance the benefits of committing such crimes against the potential costs of being punished for their criminal behavior either by their state authorities or by the ICC. Specifically, soldiers will commit a crime if the benefits associated with it are higher than the probability of conviction multiplied by the punishment they expect to receive.[11]

State authorities are also faced with a choice, a choice between prosecuting or not prosecuting soldiers who committed crimes. The state may benefit from prosecuting some crimes because prosecution improves military discipline, increases the chances for peace, or promotes the legitimacy of the state worldwide. But prosecution can also be damaging for the state: It may lower public morale, generate opposition, or expose facts that the state would rather hide. If the costs of prosecution for the state outweigh the benefits, the state would not prosecute without some pressure from the ICC.

The pressure exerted by the ICC is different depending on the chosen rule of admissibility: complementarity or primacy. Under complementarity, the state has an incentive to prosecute its soldiers because that would preempt the ICC from intervening and embarrassing the state.

[11] *See* A. Mitchell Polinsky & Steven Shavell, *The Economic Theory of Public Enforcement of Law*, 38 J. ECON. LIT. 45, 47–48 (2000) (presenting this simple model of criminal behavior).

Under primacy, the state has no incentive to prosecute, because the ICC would be able to take over the case all the way until it is concluded.

If the state is expected to prosecute its soldiers, soldiers will be deterred, but only if this prosecution is genuine. It is useful to divide states into two groups: "rule of law states" and "corrupt states." Rule of law states are states with a functioning judicial system. These states do not investigate all suspects, but when they do start an investigation, this investigation will inevitably be genuine. If the investigation confirms suspects of a crime, it will lead to a fair and legitimate trial, and if the accused really is guilty, he will be subject to conviction and a penalty that suits the severity of his crimes. Corrupt states, in contrast, have a dysfunctional judicial system. In these states, the police, prosecutors, or even judges may be pressured by politicians or by public opinion to conduct a sham investigation or a sham trial. Proceedings in these countries may be unnecessarily delayed, and investigations may be closed without a real attempt to confirm the crimes of suspects. Sometimes trials will result in false acquittals or unjustifiably low penalties.

Complementarity leads to more deterrence than primacy in rule of law states, because complementarity gives those states an incentive to investigate crimes and rule of law states always conduct genuine investigations. In contrast, primacy leads to better deterrence than complementarity in corrupt states, because primacy prevents corrupt states from conducting sham investigations and shielding soldiers from the ICC. Only a complete trial for an international crime is sufficient to preempt the ICC from intervening under primacy, and this is something that corrupt states will find difficult to fake.

Scholars have suggested that the ICTY chose the rule of primacy exactly because national systems under its jurisdiction were believed to be corrupt and suspected of using sham trials.[12] Does this imply that complementarity is the superior rule for the ICC? Not necessarily. Empirical research indicates that under the ICCs jurisdiction there are both rule of law states and corrupt states.[13] This fact is easily confirmed by anyone who reads the list of the 122 members of the ICC. The list includes many of the law-abiding states of western and northern Europe,

[12] *See* Jeffrey L. Dunoff & Joel P. Trachtman, *The Law and Economics of Humanitarian Law Violations in Internal Conflict*, 93 Amer. J. Int'l L. 394, 405 (1999).

[13] *See* Simmons & Danner, Note 11, Chapter 2 at 238.

but also numerous failed regimes in Africa.[14] All these states are subject to the same admissibility rule.

To find the optimal admissibility rule for the ICC, one must add another factor into the analysis besides the types of states under the ICC's jurisdiction. This factor is the probability of prosecution by the ICC. It is useful to distinguish between two probabilities of prosecution: a high probability and a low probability. A high probability of prosecution is enough to directly deter soldiers because when multiplied by the penalty which the ICC will issue, it is higher than the benefits the soldier expects from committing the crime. In contrast, a low probability of prosecution is not enough to directly deter soldiers because when multiplied by the expected penalty, it is lower than the benefits from the crime.

Under complementarity, even a low probability of prosecution, which cannot directly deter soldiers, is enough to incentivize states to investigate the crimes of their combatants. The incentives of states are different than those of soldiers because, on the one hand, national prosecution is usually politically feasible for the state and, on the other hand, the reputational damage caused to the states whose soldiers are found guilty of war crimes by the ICC is expected to be immense. In fact, this reputational damage is expected to be so big that the United States and Russia, among other countries, decided to avoid this risk altogether by not joining the ICC's jurisdiction despite originally signing the Rome Statute.

Another factor that makes even a low probability of prosecution by the ICC enough to incentivize states to investigate their soldiers stems from the unique way in which the ICC applies complementarity. When making the decision whether to investigate a situation, the ICC would consider whether the state generally prosecutes cases of a similar kind. Once an investigation of the issue commenced, however, the ICC would avoid exercising its jurisdiction only if there are proceedings against the same person and substantially the same conduct.[15] To

[14] *See* the list of state parties at the ICC at: https://asp.icc-cpi.int/en_menus/asp/states%20parties/Pages/the%20states%20parties%20to%20the%20rome%20statute.aspx (last visited May 3, 2019).

[15] *See* Judgment on the appeal of the Republic of Kenya against the decision of Pre-trial Chamber II of May 30, 2011 entitled "Decision on the Application by the Government of Kenya Challenging the Admissibility of the Case Pursuant to Article 19(2)(b) of the Statute," *Situation in the Republic of Kenya (Muthaura, Kenyatta, and Ali)* (ICC-01/09-02/11 OA), Appeals Chamber, Aug. 30, 2011 [hereinafter Kenya Judgment] par. 38–39.

prevent the ICC from commencing an investigation under complementarity, the state has an incentive to prosecute its soldiers regularly even when the probability of ICC prosecution faced by every individual soldier is low. A low probability of prosecution vis-à-vis every soldier translates into a significant chance that an investigation against the state will be opened by the ICC. Once an investigation is opened, all soldiers that were not adequately prosecuted by the state could be targeted by the ICC, causing the state a significant reputational damage. Under complementarity, therefore, when the probability of prosecution by the ICC is low, rule of law states will prosecute their soldiers legitimately and their soldiers will be deterred. Under primacy, in contrast, rule of law states will not prosecute their soldiers. They have no incentive to prosecute because they will find it almost impossible to preempt prosecution by the ICC. Knowing this, their soldiers will expect only a low probability of prosecution by the ICC, and they will not be deterred.

In corrupt states, the picture is different under the same low probability of prosecution. Under complementarity, corrupt states will have an incentive to prosecute their soldiers, but they will only use sham investigations and sham trials to shield their soldiers from ICC prosecution. Their soldiers will consequently not be deterred. Under primacy, these states will not have any incentive to prosecute their soldiers. The soldiers will expect a low probability of prosecution by the ICC and will not be deterred from committing crimes.

All in all, when the probability of prosecution is low, complementarity is clearly superior to primacy regardless of the types of states under the ICC's jurisdiction. Complementarity leads to more deterrence than primacy in rule of law states, while in corrupt states both rules of admissibility will not deter soldiers.

This changes when the probability of prosecution is high. Under complementarity, rule of law states will prosecute their soldiers legitimately and deter them from committing crimes. Under primacy, rule of law states will not prosecute their soldiers, but the soldiers will still be deterred because they expect a high probability of prosecution by the ICC. In other words, under primacy, the soldiers are directly deterred by the ICC, regardless of the practice of national authorities.

In corrupt states, complementarity and a high probability of ICC prosecution will give states an incentive to prosecute. But corrupt states will only conduct sham prosecutions, leaving their soldiers undeterred. Under primacy, in contrast, corrupt states cannot shield their soldiers from the ICC. Soldiers who expect a high probability of prosecution by the ICC will be directly deterred.

The conclusion of this analysis is that with a high probability of prosecution, primacy is clearly superior regardless of the type of states under the ICC's jurisdiction. In rule of law states, soldiers will be equally deterred under both admissibility rules. But in corrupt states, primacy can deter soldiers where complementarity would fail.

Table 6.1 may help to clarify this dynamic further:

Table 6.1 *Deterrence under complementarity and primacy*

	Low probability of prosecution	High probability of prosecution
Rule of law states (Sham prosecution impossible)	Soldiers will be deterred only under complementarity	Soldiers will be deterred under both rules
Corrupt states (Sham prosecution possible)	Soldiers will not be deterred under any rule	Soldiers will be deterred only under primacy

What does all this mean? It means that when the type of states under the ICC's jurisdiction is unknown, or when the ICC faces a mix of states of different types, there is still a way to determine which rule is superior: complementarity or primacy. Under a low probability of prosecution, complementarity will lead to more deterrence. Under a high probability of prosecution, primacy will deter more soldiers.

Several caveats are needed when considering this analysis: First, this nonintuitive result appears because soldiers are assumed not to be deterred under a low probability of prosecution, but to be deterred under a high probability of prosecution. In real life, soldiers are not all cut from the same cloth and they face different exigencies on the battlefield. Some soldiers may not be deterred by a high probability of prosecution by the ICC, but if their state is certainly motivated to prosecute them under complementarity, this would be enough to deter them. If soldiers' quality of being deterred is taken from a wide distribution, there are bound to be soldiers like this, just as there are bound to be soldiers that will be deterred even under a low probability of prosecution. Therefore, with a wide distribution of soldiers' types, the neat result doesn't hold for all soldiers. To some extent, the ICC may be able to correct for that by tweaking the other component of deterrence – the size of the penalty – for example, by issuing higher penalties for more severe crimes. But the ability of the ICC to do that is always limited. Penalties have to be fair and not just deterring and they are capped by the maximum possible penalty in the ICC, which is life imprisonment.[16]

Second, the analysis assumes that soldiers are acting rationally. Some may argue that soldiers engaged in war crimes are often irrational.[17] But this doesn't pose a severe problem for the argument because even if every individual soldier has some unique biases that affect his decision, unless these biases are systematic and work in the same direction, the assumption of rationality will lead to the most accurate prediction of soldier's behavior.[18]

A bigger challenge is the claim that soldiers will usually not be aware of the probability, or even the possibility, of ICC prosecution. Absent this information, soldiers are unable to make a rational decision. Yet there is a good answer to this challenge. Soldiers may not know the state of the law or understand how the ICC works, but the lawyers that advise their superior officers know these things quite well. Senior officers and lawyers have a clear professional interest to prevent their soldiers from being prosecuted and severely punished. Together, they would set rules of engagement and determine norms of behavior that would direct the practices of simple soldiers and minimize the punishment they will face.[19] Thus, soldiers will be funneled to behave in a way that matches a rational calculation of the possibility of prosecution, without actually making this calculation themselves. In addition to that explanation, one should not underestimate the ability of soldiers to assess the risk of prosecution they face even without understanding legal technicalities. Soldiers read newspapers and talk to their comrades about potential

[16] Rome Statute, art. 77(1).

[17] *See* James F. Alexander, *The International Criminal Court and the Prevention of Atrocities: Predicting the Court's Impact*, 54 Vill. L. Rev. 1, 16–19 (2009).

[18] *See* Milton Friedman, *The Methodology of Positive Economics*, at Essays in Positive Economics 3, 8–9 (1953) (explaining that models should be checked by their ability to provide accurate predictions, not by the accuracy of their assumptions).

[19] *See* Amichai Cohen, *Legal Operational Advice in the Israeli Defense Forces: The International Law Department and the Changing Nature of International Humanitarian Law*, 26 Conn. J. Int'l L. 367, 398–402 (2011) (Explaining how operational legal advisers shape norms of conduct on the battlefield).

penalties. They can form some vague assessments of their chances of facing prosecution, which would translate into deterrence.

C If Sham Trials Can Be Detected

The analysis so far assumes that the ICC isn't able to expose sham trials. Indeed, sham trials are probably very difficult to expose both because of the information costs associated with monitoring the actions of state prosecution and because exposing fraudulent proceedings can lead to severe backlash of the accused states against the ICC. Under this set of assumptions, rule of law states will avoid sham trials because of the quality of their own legal system, while corrupt states may use sham trials whenever they find it worthwhile to do so.

Nevertheless, sometimes the ICC may be able to expose sham trials. Sham trials may occur either because the state is unable to conduct a real trial or because it is unwilling to do so. If the state's judicial system is so defective that it is unable to conduct trials, the threat of exposing trials as a sham may not change the practice of the state.[20] However, if the state is able to conduct genuine trials but chooses to pressure the judicial system in order to shield soldiers from the ICC, the state can be deterred from this practice, provided that sham trials can be exposed. Under complementarity, such a corrupt state would realize that conducting a genuine trial is the only way to protect its soldiers from ICC prosecution. Furthermore, if the state would conduct sham trials, the ICC would declare that the state is unwilling to prosecute its soldiers. This declaration itself would be very damaging to the state's reputation.[21]

If sham trials can be exposed, complementarity is therefore the superior rule. Both corrupt and rule of law states will not conduct sham trials if they can be exposed by the ICC. This implies that a low probability of prosecution would suffice to give both types of states an incentive to prosecute their soldiers, who would consequently be deterred.

If the probability of prosecution is high, soldiers would be deterred under both rules: under primacy because they fear direct ICC prosecution and under complementarity because they expect to face a genuine trial by their state. But even when the probability of prosecution is high, complementarity is a more efficient rule. Complementarity would delegate most of the work to national systems, who would adopt the

[20] *See* Kleffner, Note 35, Chapter 4 at 321.
[21] *See id* at 320.

legislation and the judicial practices that are necessary to ensure genuine national prosecution.

If the ICC has a credible threat to expose all sham trials, then it would never have to execute this threat. States would never use sham trials in order to avoid the reputational cost associated with exposing a trial as a sham. It may be, however, that the ICC is limited in its ability to expose sham trials. Because exposing sham trials is expensive and difficult, the ICC may be able to expose only some of the sham trials, which implies that states face only a limited probability that their sham trials will be exposed. Corrupt states would conduct sham trials if the advantages of a sham trial in their eyes outweigh the reputational costs of being exposed as conducting sham trials multiplied by the probability of exposure. Under this set of assumptions, complementarity may lead to lower deterrence in corrupt states, because these states will still use sham trials, at least some of the time.

The most realistic set of assumptions would consider that the ICC has a limited amount of resources, both in terms of the abilities of its staff and in terms of the goodwill of the states under its jurisdiction. Every time the ICC prosecutes a case it uses some of these resources, and every time the ICC exposes a trial as a sham it uses resources from the same pool. In fact, exposing a sham trial probably uses more resources than prosecuting a case, although it is impossible to stipulate exactly how much more. To optimize deterrence, the ICC has to choose the optimal mix of actions – prosecuting new cases and exposing sham trials.

Under complementarity, the ICC would spend some of its resources prosecuting new cases and some of its resources exposing sham trials. Soldiers will be deterred if the probability of prosecution by the ICC is high enough to motivate states to prosecute and the chances of exposing sham trials are high enough to motivate states to conduct genuine trials. Under primacy, in contrast, the states do not have an incentive to prosecute and the ICC would spend all of its resources prosecuting new cases. If the ICC has enough resources to reach a high probability of prosecution, soldiers will be directly deterred. If the probability of ICC prosecution is low, soldiers will not be deterred because they know their own state will not prosecute them.

To state definitively which rule, complementarity or primacy, would lead to better deterrence under these conditions, a set of factors needs to be observed. Relevant factors include: the number of corrupt and rule of law states under the ICC's jurisdiction, the number of potential criminals in these states, the costs of prosecuting cases, the costs of exposing sham trials, the reputational sanction caused to the state when the ICC prosecutes one of its soldiers, and the reputational sanction caused to the state when its trial is exposed as a sham.

Evidently, the task of determining which admissibility rule would lead to better deterrence depends on facts that only a complex empirical investigation can reveal. The assumption that sham trials cannot be exposed may not be 100 percent accurate, but it is quite reasonable and simplifies the analysis immensely. Therefore, while an exact prediction of the prospects of deterrence is still impossible, proceeding under the assumption that sham trials cannot be exposed seems like the best way forward to find the optimal rule of admissibility. This route is followed by the next section.

D Normative Solutions

So far, the analysis revealed that if sham trials cannot be exposed, complementarity leads to better deterrence when the probability of ICC prosecution is low, and primacy leads to better deterrence when the probability of ICC prosecution is high. The reason is that under a low probability of prosecution, soldiers in rule of law states would be deterred only under complementarity, while soldiers in corrupt states would not be deterred under both rules. Under a high probability of prosecution, soldiers in rule of law states would be deterred under both rules, while soldiers in corrupt states would be deterred only under primacy. The task of this section is to translate this analysis to concrete normative solutions that are aimed at maximizing the deterrence of soldiers.

1 Amending the Rome Statute over Time

Few would dispute that the probability of prosecution by the ICC more than sixteen years after its creation is low. Therefore, complementarity remains the preferable rule of admissibility. In the future, this may change. The ICC may improve its efficiency and reach a high probability of prosecution of war criminals. If and when this happens, changing the rule of admissibility from complementarity to primacy would optimize deterrence.

Amending the Rome Statute to change the admissibility rule may be difficult, but it is certainly possible. Any state party is able to propose amendments to the Rome Statute that would be considered by the Assembly of the State Parties. The Assembly can accept the amendment with a two-thirds majority. An amendment shall enter into force for all state parties a year after seven-eighths of the state parties ratified or accepted the amendment.[22] Unfortunately, one can expect that some countries will resist a shift from complementarity to primacy, rendering this solution difficult to implement.

2 *Changing the Admissibility Rule by the ICC*

The rule of admissibility applied by the ICC is determined by the Rome Statute, which, as explained previously, can be difficult to amend. But the Rome Statute is vague enough to allow the ICC some level of judicial discretion. ICC judges can use this discretion to change the interpretation of the admissibility rule in ways that are conducive to deterrence.

Complementarity prevents the ICC from assuming jurisdiction if the state conducted an investigation and followed it through with prosecution or, alternatively, decided not to prosecute. This definition begs the question what counts as an "investigation." The word is broad enough to encompass several interpretations. The ICC can choose the proper interpretation to maximize deterrence. When the probability of prosecution is low, the ICC can determine that even basic forensic actions would constitute investigation, in order to give states an incentive to act. When the probability of prosecution is high, the ICC can require significant and expensive actions to form an investigation that could preempt it from exercising jurisdiction. In this way, the ICC could decrease the chances of sham investigations without actually having to point to misconduct by the state. Setting a higher bar to state investigations could transform the existing rule of complementarity into a rule similar to primacy.

Some cases of the ICC demonstrate how it can require high standards from state proceedings without branding the state directly as engaged in deception. In one case, the Appeals Chamber of the ICC decided that only specific steps such as "interviewing witnesses or suspects, collecting documentary evidence, or carrying out forensic analyses" taken to ascertain whether the suspect committed the conduct alleged by the ICC would qualify as an investigation. Mere plans to take these steps or taking such steps only against other suspects wouldn't count as an investigation.[23] The crucial thing stressed by the ICC judgment is that the determination whether there was an investigation at all is distinct from the

[22] *See* Rome Statute, art. 121.
[23] *See* Kenya Judgment, Note 15, at 3.

decision whether an existing investigation is legitimate.[24] This allows the ICC to set a clear bar for what constitutes an investigation without having to accuse the state of misconduct and risk political backlash.

The ICC followed the same course in a decision issued regarding the case of Saif Al-Islam Gaddafi. According to the decision, the state bears the burden of proving it conducted an investigation. The ICC demanded specific information about the investigation conducted in Libya and about Libyan law.[25] Requiring a high threshold of domestic proceedings from the state is not only useful in preventing sham investigations that do not deter soldiers; they can also assure the ICC that the basic rights of the accused are observed. This was probably the ICC's main concern in this case.

If the probability of prosecution by the ICC improves in the future, this line of cases can be followed by setting increasingly stringent standards for what constitutes an investigation. This method would shift the admissibility rule from complementarity to primacy without the need for treaty amendment.

3 *Adopting a Two-Tiered System*

The main problem addressed by this chapter is the fact that the ICC faces both corrupt states and rule of law states with the same admissibility rule. Changing the rule of admissibility conditioned on the probability of prosecution may solve this problem because, under certain conditions, it can increase deterrence in one type of states without reducing it in the other. But one can imagine a different solution to this problem: adopting two different admissibility rules and sorting each type of states into the rule that maximizes the deterrence of its soldiers.

How can this be done? The most reasonable way is to draft an additional protocol for the Rome Statute that would apply the rule of primacy. States that join only the Rome statute itself would continue to be subject to complementarity as before, but states that ratify the additional protocol would be subject to primacy. Now the only problem that remains is sorting states into the right regime – the admissibility rule that will maximize deterrence of their soldiers. Ultimately, states are the ones

[24] *See id*, at 15.

[25] *See* Prosecutor v. Saif Al-Islam Gaddafi & Abdullah Al-Senussi, Case No. ICC-01/11-01/11, Pre-trial Chamber I Decision Requesting Further Submissions on Issues Related to the Admissibility of the Case against Saif Al-Islam Gaddafi, 5–19 (Dec. 7, 2012).

making the choice between the regimes. Therefore, the challenge is to adopt rules that would incentivize states to choose the right admissibility rule themselves.

Deterrence would be maximized if rule of law states would remain in the default complementarity regime and corrupt states would join the protocol that applies primacy. How can each type of states be prompted to choose the right regime? That all depends on what states are trying to achieve. Some scholars argue that states actually want to prevent their soldiers from committing crimes and that is why they join the ICC's jurisdiction.[26] If that is the case, the work of drafting the additional protocol is very easy indeed. Rule of law states would choose to stay in the complementarity regime of their own accord to maximize the deterrence of their soldiers, while corrupt states would opt for the primacy protocol for exactly the same reason.

If states are not only seeking to enhance the deterrence of their soldiers, the right regime has to be sold to each type of states according to its own interests. For example, imagine that corrupt states usually have bad reputations for human rights compliance and are therefore looking for ways to signal their commitment to the international community by joining strict human rights regimes.[27] In that case, the primacy protocol could be presented as a more stringent regime to draw in more corrupt states than rule of law states. Because primacy is inherently more constraining on states' sovereignty, selling it to corrupt states as a demanding regime – that can improve their reputation when they join it – should be done quite easily.

Alternatively, the primacy protocol can include other provisions that have nothing to do with admissibility, but are appealing to corrupt states for entirely different reasons. The protocol will be sold to corrupt states as part of a "package deal," bundling together provisions that suit their interests with the primacy rule, which would maximize the deterrence of their soldiers.

If a two-tiered system is adopted, some corrupt states may still lag behind and fail to join the primacy protocol. In that case, if the court would reach a high probability of prosecution, it may be beneficial to amend the Rome Statute and to set primacy as the sole rule of admissibility. The more states join the primacy protocol, the greater the pressure

[26] *See* Simmons & Danner, Note 11, Chapter 2 at 234.

[27] *See* Hathaway, Note 45, Chapter 5 at 510–511.

that other states will face to follow suit. Eventually, it would also become more politically feasible to formally amend the Rome Statute and adopt primacy as the binding rule for all member states.

4 Distinguishing between States' Types

So far, the analysis has assumed that the ICC cannot treat differently corrupt states and rule of law states. It may seem intuitive that if the ICC could focus its resources on a specific type of states, deterrence would be reached. Unfortunately, increasing the probability of prosecution in only one type of states would not deter all soldiers. If the ICC reaches a high probability of prosecution in corrupt states and only a low probability of prosecution in rule of law states, some soldiers will not be deterred under both rules: Under complementarity, soldiers in corrupt states will not be deterred; under primacy, soldiers in rule of law states will not be deterred. If the court manages instead to reach a high probability of prosecution in rule of law states while sustaining only a low probability of prosecution in corrupt states, soldiers in corrupt states will not be deterred under both admissibility rules.

If the ICC is able to treat states differently conditioned on their type, it may decide to use its interpretive discretion and apply a different admissibility rule to different types of states. As suggested previously, the ICC may be able to shift the admissibility rule by interpretative discretion: requiring so much for an investigation to preempt it from prosecution that the rule of complementarity would function in fact like primacy. All the ICC has to do to optimize deterrence is to apply normal complementarity to rule of law states and the stricter standard resembling primacy to corrupt states.

While this solution may seem perfect, it can be very dangerous to perform. If the ICC applies different admissibility standards openly to different states, it would appear biased and this can damage its legitimacy. The court is already facing allegations for an unmerited focus on African states. Admitting that the court discriminates between types of states can lead to a devastating backlash. The only reasonable option for the court is to try to hide the fact that it applies different standards to different states. This will lead to judgments that are unpredictable and inconsistent, damaging both the ability of the court to deter soldiers – who wouldn't know in advance what rule of admissibility would be applied – and the support for the court in the international community.

E How Complementarity Affects States' Willingness to Join the Court's Jurisdiction

Today, the ICC's jurisdiction covers a mix of rule of law states and corrupt states. The normative recommendations discussed in the previous section suggest ways to improve deterrence considering the current mix of states. But the mix of states under the ICC's jurisdiction can change. States can decide whether to join the ICC or not conditioned on whether they are satisfied with the admissibility rule. States can also leave the ICC if they are dissatisfied with it, as Burundi and the Philippines already did.[28]

If states wish to deter their own soldiers from committing crimes, they are more likely to join the ICC's jurisdiction if the admissibility rule leads to the deterrence of their soldiers. Rule of law states are more likely to join the ICC under complementarity and corrupt states are more likely to join the court's jurisdiction under primacy.

Another possibility discussed previously is that states join the ICC in order to get some reputational benefit. But the reputational benefit of joining the ICC's jurisdiction must be balanced against the reputational costs generated by the prosecution of soldiers from the same state. Every soldier that is prosecuted indicates that the state was engaged in war crimes and this damages the state's reputation. For that reason, even if the state cares only about its reputation and not about preventing crimes, it must be interested in deterrence, because deterred soldiers do not commit crimes that can harm the state's reputation.

If the probability of prosecution by the ICC is low, rule of law states are more likely to join the ICC's jurisdiction under complementarity. Only under complementarity will soldiers be deterred and commit no crimes that would translate to a reputational damage for the state. The state gains the reputational benefit associated with joining the ICC and loses nothing.

In corrupt states under a low probability of ICC prosecution, soldiers will not be deterred both under complementarity and under primacy. But under complementarity, the state can choose to shield its soldiers with sham investigations. While sham investigations and trials may be costly, the state will choose to use them any time they cost less than the

[28] *See* Jason Gutierrez, *Philippines Officially Leaves the International Criminal Court*, The N. Y. Times Mar. 17, 2019, available at: www.nytimes.com/2019/03/17/world/asia/philippines-international-criminal-court.html.

reputational costs of having its crimes exposed by the ICC. In contrast, under primacy, soldiers in corrupt states will still not be deterred, but the state would not be able to shield them by sham trials and would face the reputational costs of ICC prosecution. Corrupt states would prefer to join the ICC under complementarity because they would earn reputation by ratifying the Rome Statute and face lower future costs.

It appears that when the probability of prosecution is low, both rule of law states and corrupt states have a greater interest in joining the ICC under complementarity. Indeed, the probability of prosecution by the ICC was certainly low in its first years, and adopting the rule of complementarity may be partly accountable for the high number of both rule of law states and corrupt states that joined the ICC's jurisdiction. While many believed in 1998 that it would take a decade or more before the first sixty states ratified the Rome Statute and allowed it to enter into force, this threshold was reached as early as April 2002.[29] Several years later, the number of state parties exceeded 120.

If the probability of ICC prosecution becomes high, rule of law states will join the ICC either under complementarity or under primacy. In both cases, these states will gain reputation from joining the court and because their soldiers will be deterred they do not expect any later reputational losses.

In contrast, corrupt states must consider that even with a high probability of prosecution their soldiers will still commit crimes if the rule of complementarity is chosen. Corrupt states will be forced to conduct costly sham trials in every case in which they want to avoid ICC prosecution and the reputational damage associated with it. Under primacy, soldiers in corrupt states will be deterred and will not commit crimes, saving the state the expense and risks that are the result of sham trials.

This implies that, to the extent the ICC wishes to draw in as many states as possible under its jurisdiction, primacy is the superior rule under a high probability of prosecution. Complementarity may have been a better rule for an incipient court with a low probability of prosecution, but if in the future the court's ability to prosecute would be significantly improved, shifting to primacy may be a good idea.

[29] *See* Dominic McGoldrick, *Criminal Trials before International Tribunals: Legality and Legitimacy in* The Permanent International Criminal Court: Legal and Policy Issues (Studies in International Law) (Eric Donnelly, Dominic McGoldrick, and Peter J. Rowe, eds.) 9 at 43.

This analysis applies only under certain restricting conditions. For example, the analysis assumes that states earn the same amount of reputation for joining the ICC's jurisdiction under a complementarity regime and under a primacy regime. But it is possible that joining a primacy regime will lead to a greater reputational benefit than joining a complementarity regime because it involves a greater concession of sovereignty. The analysis also assumes that soldiers are directly deterred by a high probability of prosecution and not deterred under a low probability of prosecution. As explained previously, when soldiers have different utility functions, this doesn't always apply. Some soldiers would still commit crimes under a high probability of prosecution even if they cannot be shielded. States may consider this when they decide whether to join the ICC's jurisdiction. The analysis also assumes that the ICC doesn't make any mistakes and doesn't prosecute innocent soldiers. The truth may be different. If the ICC can make mistakes, or if it is biased against certain states, states may be motivated not to join its jurisdiction.

The key to the analysis in this chapter is realizing that the rules regulating the intervention of the ICC in domestic affairs do not only determine when the ICC would produce a legal solution, a solution that could be better or worse than the solutions states adopt on their own. Rather, states and their soldiers operate in the shadow of the ICC and they will change their behavior conditioned on the chosen rule of admissibility. This section takes the analysis one step forward. It explains that the number and the character of states under the ICC jurisdiction will depend on the chosen rule of admissibility. This final consideration – taking into account the incentive of states to join the jurisdiction of an international court – is not unique to criminal courts. Section 2.D explained that if international courts increase their intervention in domestic affairs, states may choose not to join, or to exit, their jurisdiction. That is something international courts must be aware of.

The ICC should care not only about the number of states under its jurisdiction but also about the type of these states. For example, the ICC may want to draw in rule of law states to increase the support for the court in rich and influential power centers. Alternatively, the ICC may want to draw in corrupt states because these states may be involved in more international crimes of the type the ICC wishes to prosecute or to deter. These strategic calculations may shift over the lifespan of the ICC. Some periods may call for more support from well-behaving states while in other periods the ICC would like to increase the volume of the cases it processes.

F Conclusion

Does the ICC deter international crimes? The analysis in this chapter assumes rational behavior by soldiers and by state authorities and concludes that the answer to this question depends on the rule of admissibility chosen by the ICC. The level of ICC intervention should be regulated with reference to its ability to deter international crimes. Specifically, when the probability of prosecution by the ICC is low, complementarity can deter more crimes and increase the number of states under the ICC's jurisdiction. Under a high probability of ICC prosecution, primacy leads to better deterrence and would motivate more states to join the ICC.

The ability of the ICC to pose a real threat of prosecution for soldiers is, for now, very limited. This may change in the future. The example of the ECHR demonstrates that an international court can shift from a handful of cases a year to thousands. But this is unlikely to happen soon; in fact, it may never happen. Fortunately, there are three reasons why the ICC probably has a much stronger effect on reducing international crimes than either direct deterrence of soldiers or motivating states to prosecute would generate.

First, as mentioned in Subsection 4.A.1, the ICC created a powerful myth, a myth that somewhere in The Hague there is a court that would eventually bring war criminals to justice. Soldiers and militia members all over the world are exposed to that myth, and it may affect their behavior. These soldiers may not engage in rational cost-benefit calculations, but the constant threat of international prosecution and the humiliation involved in justifying their actions to judges and lawyers may constrain some of their actions.

Second, states that joined the ICC's jurisdiction have often reviewed and amended their criminal codes to conform with the Rome Statute. Scholars have argued that states do this because they are afraid the court will find them unable to prosecute their own soldiers for lack of appropriate legislation.[30] In this way, complementarity doesn't just shape the interest of states to investigate crimes that were already committed. It has

[30] *See* KLEFFNER, Note 35, Chapter 4 At 333–337.

a much greater and lasting effect – changing the internal criminal laws of states in ways that may prevent future crimes.

Finally, states are increasingly taking another measure to preempt ICC prosecution. They are investing enormous resources in legal experts that would advise all levels of the state's hierarchy from politicians to soldiers on the field. Scholars have argued that the growing involvement of lawyers is not necessarily an unmitigated good. Creating a bureaucracy of legal authorization may numb the ability of soldiers to exercise personal and emotional judgment and lead to more rather than fewer war crimes.[31] Nevertheless, one shouldn't underestimate the long-term effect that a large body of trained lawyers has on the governance of states.[32] The lawyers that were placed to defend the state from the threat of international prosecution may end up defending it from itself. They will be the ones that will fight for legality and the rule of law in all aspects of the state's behavior.

And the story doesn't end there. The institutions and trained lawyers that emerge in different states tend to influence their peers in neighbor countries. Scholars have noted that the norm of accountability for international crimes spreads from one country to the other through a growing network of lawyers and activists.[33]

[31] *See* Bassok, Note 53, Chapter 4.

[32] *See* Halliday, Karpik & Feeley, Note 52, Chapter 4 at 1–9.

[33] *See* Kathryn Sikkink, The Justice Cascade: How Human Rights Prosecutions Are Changing World Politics 248–253 (2011).

7

Conclusions

If you want to understand international courts, you mustn't observe them in isolation. You must study them in their natural environment, surrounded by other actors such as states, NGOs, national courts, parliaments, and even individuals. The influence of international courts on the world depends on the interests and the incentives of these other actors.

Once it is accepted that international courts are not all-mighty dictators, one can see that the international arena is actually a complicated system of checks and balances. The constant conflict between international courts and other institutions may sometimes be wasteful, but it is the only way to prevent a few powerful people from taking over the world. In a globalized world, the lessons that Montesquieu and James Madison taught about the importance of friction between branches of government need to be applied to the international arena as well.

The chapter addresses this challenge from several angles. First, it highlights the parallels between the theories presented in this book to support intervention by international courts and theories used to justify domestic judicial review. Then, it explains the role of international courts in light of theories of globalization. Finally, the ways in which international courts overcome some persistent difficulties are briefly examined.

A International and Domestic Judicial Review

The arguments against domestic judicial review were divided by scholars into two types.[1] The first type of arguments is focused on the legitimacy of the decision-making process. For example, such an argument would doubt whether it is legitimate to let an unelected court change the

[1] *See* Jeremy Waldron, *The Core of the Case against Judicial Review*, 115 YALE L.J. 1346, 1372–1373 (2006) (proposing this division).

decisions of an elected parliament.[2] The second type of argument is focused on outcomes. It questions, for example, whether a court is actually able to reach a decision that has better consequences than a decision made by a parliament equipped with the capacity to make wise decisions.[3]

The arguments made in this book largely track the distinction between a focus on process and a focus on outcomes. The only chapter that targets the legitimacy of the process instead of the consequences of judicial intervention is Chapter 2. This chapter argues that deferring to the decisions of states is sometimes mandated by the fact that states are usually the best representatives of all individuals affected by their policies. But there are cases in which states cannot be trusted to represent the interests of the people they influence. These cases are known as "democratic failures." They involve the rights of foreigners; disenfranchised people such as prisoners; discrete and insular minorities; and groups that cannot defend their rights against the stronger power of small interest groups. In these cases, international courts should not grant states a margin of appreciation. The literature on domestic judicial review has argued that in cases that involve such groups elected bodies are not truly representative and judicial intervention is justified – laying the theoretical foundations on which Chapter 2 stands.[4]

Just like democratic states do not always give a fair share of political capital to every person, Chapter 2 highlights that the negotiations leading to international treaties can give an unfair advantage to some countries over others. Specifically, countries that have a credible threat to leave the negotiation table can extort large concessions from countries that are committed to the success of the treaty. If all states need to agree to an amending protocol of an existing treaty, countries that resist change gain a potent veto power. International courts that use expansive interpretation bend the text that results from the collective decision-making of states. International courts are justified in doing so – much like domestic courts that overrule parliaments – because mechanisms of collective decision-making are sometimes imperfect.

[2] *See* Alexander M. Bickel, The Least Dangerous Branch – The Supreme Court at the Bar of Politics 16–17 (2d ed., 1986).

[3] *See e.g.* Adrian Vermeule, Law and the Limits of Reason 83, 90 (2009) (mentioning factors that give legislatures a decisional advantage over courts according to the Condorcet Jury Theorem).

[4] *See generally* Ely, Note 71, Chapter 2.

Chapter 3 starts to investigate the outcomes of intervention by international courts. The argument there may seem simple – international courts are better able to use the decisional advantages of comparative law than national courts. However, it is crucial to understand that this advantage doesn't stem from greater expertise or sophistication of international judges over domestic judges. The advantage of international courts is in their institutional position, which allows them to tap into the benefits of the Condorcet Jury Theorem. If international courts follow the policies made by most national courts, who, in turn, make their policies independently, they can make good decisions. These decisions can then be adopted by states under the court's jurisdiction.

A parallel to theories of domestic judicial review isn't immediately apparent. Scholars have investigated some advantages that stem directly from the institutional position of national courts, as opposed to the proficiency of the judges within them. For example, scholars have reviewed, and criticized, the proposition that because common law courts deal with specific cases they have a decisional advantage over political bodies that make policy in the abstract.[5] But the advantage international courts possess according to Chapter 3 is somewhat different. It is the location of international courts in a long series of decision-makers that gives them their unique capacity: the ability to aggregate the decisions of many national courts without creating an information cascade. The advantage of international courts depends not only on their own behavior. It also depends on the conduct of the states under their jurisdiction and their national courts. To succeed, international courts must shape the behavior of other actors by giving them the right incentives. Chapter 3 argues that a strategic use of the margin of appreciation doctrine can achieve that goal.

Chapter 4 starts to assess the impact of international courts after a judgment was already issued. The chapter isn't concerned with the content of the judgment itself, but rather with its impact on democratic processes. One can imagine that taking away decisions from the public and transferring them to a small group of experts could seriously harm public deliberation. Public debate complies with the worn adage "use it or lose it." If the people are excluded from important decisions, they will forfeit the ability to argue effectively and to decide for themselves.

[5] *See generally* Frederick Schauer, *Do Cases Make Bad Law?* 73 UNI CHI. L. REV 883 (2006).

But international courts do not block public deliberation, argues Chapter 4. Because a judgment is never the final word on the matter, it opens the door for deliberation later on. For a series of reasons mentioned in the chapter, this deliberation is likely to be even better than if international courts kept out of the issue completely.

International courts shift public discourse from a language of interests to a language of rights. Through their reasoned judgments, courts guide the public toward a method of argument based on principles and values, not on naked power. This quality of judicial decision-making was suggested by scholars as a justification for domestic judicial review.[6] Scholars have explored the ways in which judges apply principles to specific facts, giving public values the necessary depth that would allow them to infuse the public discourse.[7]

International courts are likely to face political backlash to some of their decisions. Backlash is usually something international courts try to avoid, but it may have beneficial side effects for public deliberation. When political bodies collide, information is generated and spreads to the public. Friction between institutions can therefore prevent the capture of power by interest groups, equipped with superior information compared to the rest of the public. The advantage of courts as instigators of friction between political bodies has already been noted by scholars studying domestic judicial review.[8]

Chapter 4 also exposes mechanisms that allow international courts to efficiently spread information within a large network of lawyers, activists, and academics. While Chapter 4 is focused on the amount of information that flows within the network, Chapter 5 uses empirical research to examine its quality. Research reveals that, at least in some settings, the network that surrounds international courts improves the accuracy of information about state noncompliance with international law. Insights from the growing field of Social Network Analysis clarify why international courts are able to augment the power of social networks as disseminators of information.

Scholars investigating domestic judicial review have voiced concern over judicial intervention in issues that can generate unpredictable chain reactions involving numerous other actors. Such issues were described as "polycentric." When the court pulls the spider web of social connections

[6] *See generally* Michelman, Note 8, Chapter 4.
[7] *See generally* Fiss, Foreword: The Forms of Justice, Note 9, Chapter 4.
[8] *See generally* Benvenisti, Judicial Review and Democratic Failures Note 85, Chapter 2.

with its many centers of power, there is no telling what the final outcome on society would be.[9] Chapter 5 provides a preliminary answer to this problem as far as the social network of human rights activists enforcing ECHR judgments is concerned. In this particular spider web, the initial push provided by an international court is likely to lead to sensible shaming efforts based on good information.

Chapter 5 raises another concern, that of undue influence on the judicial decision itself by litigating parties. Scholarship on domestic judicial review has highlighted that procedural aspects of judicial decision-making fortify it against some risks of capture. At a minimum, the advantages of courts make them better suited to resist political pressures than other plausible alternatives.[10] Chapter 5 reviews procedures for the intervention of NGOs in international courts' proceedings. While it argues that such intervention poses certain risks, it also highlights the benefits that NGOs bring to the table. Just like the literature on domestic judicial review, the chapter exposes the aspects that make international courts well-suited to withstand some pressures, but doesn't ignore their vulnerabilities. Different types of international courts are recommended different procedures to maximize the advantages of NGO intervention.

Chapter 6 analyzes the implications of the principle of complementarity applied by the ICC. The analysis there is inspired by Game Theory and uses a simple tool known as backward induction. It calculates whether the state will prosecute its soldiers conditioned on the probability of ICC prosecution and tests whether these possibilities of prosecution would deter soldiers from committing crimes to begin with. The analysis can even be pushed another step backward to check whether states would join the ICC jurisdiction conditioned on whether their soldiers will later commit crimes or not.

Scholars of domestic judicial review used similar forms of strategic analysis to investigate the implications of judicial intervention. They realized that judicial review can change the incentives of other government branches in nonintuitive ways.[11] They also showed how sequential

9 Lon L. Fuller, *The Forms and Limits of Adjudication*, 92 HARV. L. REV. 353, 394–395 (1978).

10 Abram Chayes, *The Role of the Judge in Public Law Litigation*, 89 HARV. L. REV. 1281, 1307–1312 (1976).

11 *See* James B. Thayer, *The Origin and Scope of the American Doctrine of Constitutional Law*, 7 HARV. L. REV. 129, 155–156 (1893) (arguing that a legislature aware of the possibility of judicial review would focus on questions of legality as opposed to justice

games involving multiple strategic players can ensue after a national court issues its decision.[12]

Chapter 6 demonstrates how a fear of harmful intervention by international courts may actually help states commit to prosecuting their own soldiers. States may want to sustain this commitment when they join the court's jurisdiction, even if after their soldiers commit a crime they would prefer not to act unless they were threatened by international prosecution. Similarly, scholars of domestic judicial review have already highlighted that governments want to be bound by their national courts – giving away their freedom in exchange for commitment to certain values and principles.[13]

Much can be learned from theories of domestic judicial review on the proper role of international courts. Nevertheless, international courts present an entirely different set of challenges than national courts. To appreciate the unique circumstances faced by international courts today, the nature of the international system must be investigated.

B International Courts and the International System

One cannot study a complicated problem like the nature of the global arena as a solitary intellectual. A scholar's view of such problems is inevitably shaped by paradigms shared with the scientific community.[14] This chapter describes three competing paradigms for understanding the way international law works: A Westphalian Paradigm, A Hierarchical Paradigm, and a Network Paradigm.[15] The first two paradigms may have described the role of international courts well in the past, but today international courts have to be understood as part of a network.

and not be as careful to avoid mistakes knowing that they can be corrected by the court later on).

12 *See generally* William N. Eskridge, Jr., *Reneging on History? Playing the Court/Congress/President Civil Rights Game*, 79 CAL. L. REV. 613, 644 (1991).

13 *See generally* Or Bassok & Yoav Dotan, *Solving the Countermajoritarian Difficulty?* 11 INT'L J. CONN. LAW 13 (2013).

14 *See generally* THOMAS KUHN, THE STRUCTURE OF SCIENTIFIC REVOLUTIONS (1962).

15 The distinction between these three paradigms is based on Dirk Pulkowski, *Structural Paradigms of International Law, in* THE SHIFTING ALLOCATION OF AUTHORITY IN INTERNATIONAL LAW: CONSIDERING SOVEREIGNTY, SUPREMACY AND SUBSIDIARITY 51 (Tomer Broude & Yuval Shany, eds., 2008). I changed the name of the third paradigm from the Heterarchical Paradigm to the Network Paradigm to account for the importance of social networks in understanding the world today.

The Westphalian paradigm – named after the 1648 Peace of Westphalia – is the classical way of understanding international law. Under this paradigm, states are distinct and autonomous entities with the right to zealously protect their sovereignty. They can take upon themselves legal obligations, but they are only constrained to comply with duties they willingly accepted.[16]

If states are rationally seeking to further their interests vis-à-vis other states, what role is there for international law? Scholars have argued that International law may be observed either because it suits states' individual interests, it helps states coordinate on agreed solutions, it is sustained by mutual threats to use force, or it is coerced by one powerful state on others.[17] International courts can play an important role in facilitating these functions of international law. For example, scholars argued that ICJ judgments allow states to make rational compromises resisted by their public without taking the blame for them.[18] Others have highlighted that the ICJ can help states coordinate their behavior and avoid unnecessary conflicts.[19]

But the Westphalian paradigm is ill-equipped to explain the practice of a court like the ECHR. While scholars have already noted that even the ICJ and its predecessor, the PCIJ, expansively interpreted states' treaty obligations,[20] the ECHR has raised expansive interpretation to a whole new level. The ECHR cannot be explained as a way to coordinate the actions of independent and sovereign states. It is better viewed as a proto-constitutional court that tries to improve the protection of human rights across Europe.[21]

The ECHR can be explained as part of the Hierarchical Paradigm: It imposes on states legal principles from above. If international courts are regularly ordering states to improve their behavior, it isn't surprising that scholars focused on compliance with international courts as the ultimate

[16] *See* Tom Ginsburg, *Eastphalia as the Perfection of Westphalia*, 17 IND. J. GLOBAL LEGAL STUD. 27, 29–30 (2010).

[17] *See* JACK L. GOLDSMITH & ERIC A. POSNER, THE LIMITS OF INTERNATIONAL LAW 11–12 (2005(.

[18] *See* HERSCH LAUTERPACHT, THE DEVELOPMENT OF INTERNATIONAL LAW BY THE INTERNATIONAL COURT 4 (1958).

[19] *See generally* Ginsburg & McAdams, Note 31, Chapter 4.

[20] *See* Lauterpacht, Note 26, Chapter 2 at 67.

[21] *See* Joshua L. Jackson, *Broniowski v. Poland: A Recipe for Increased Legitimacy of the European Court of Human Rights as a Supranational Constitutional Court*, 39 CONN. L. REV. 759, 777–781 (2006).

measure of their success. The ECHR and the ECJ were sold as models for international courts all over the world simply because they were effective – states actually complied with their judgments.[22]

The truth is that neither the Westphalian Paradigm nor the Hierarchical Paradigm can be categorically discarded. International law is shaped by the policy of interest-driven states and by binding rules at the same time. Scholars have noted the dissonance between these two aspects of international law. This is a contradiction that cannot be resolved.[23]

Despite the fact that many things can still be explained by the older paradigms of international law, to fully grasp the role of international law today a wholly different paradigm is needed. This is the Network Paradigm.[24] The Network Paradigm calls attention to two phenomena: first, the centers of political power around the world are becoming more and more connected; second, transnational connections are starting to form between lower levels of the states' hierarchy.

Scholars have noted that in today's globalized world, states are increasingly interdependent. The numerous links and influences between nations require the international community to narrow down states' ability to independently exercise their sovereignty.[25] Furthermore, states are no longer communicating only via diplomats who serve the wishes of the highest echelons of government. Instead, scholars have shown that mid-level state officials – bureaucrats, judges, army officers, and others – are directly communicating with their parallels across the border.[26]

Because of these two developments, the global arena resembles a complicated network with many centers of power. This is an informal network that arises spontaneously out of connections between individuals. But in order to regulate this arena, international organizations created an elaborate formal network of institutions that are tasked with maintaining global governance.[27] Studies in Social Network Analysis have suggested that formal and informal networks determine together

[22] *See generally* Helfer & Slaughter, Note 22, Chapter 3.

[23] *See generally* Martti Koskenniemi, *The Politics of International Law*, 1 Eur. J. Int'l L. 4 (1990).

[24] *See* Anne-Marie Slaughter, The Chessboard and the Web: Strategies of Connection in a Networked World 7–10 (2017).

[25] *See generally* Eyal Benvenisti, *Sovereigns as Trustees of Humanity: On the Accountability of States to Foreign Stakeholders*, 107 Amer. J. Int'l L. 295 (2013).

[26] *See generally* Slaughter, Note 23, Chapter 4.

[27] *See generally* Benvenisti, Note 18, Chapter 2.

the fate of communities.[28] International organizations are important, but so are the numerous links between people with political or economic power. This is the world of international law as it looks today.

What can international courts contribute in such a world? One of the key dangers of the tightening of informal connections between officials in different countries is that much of the important policy-making today is done under the radar of international law.[29] International courts can put policy-making back on the radar screen. They do not just order states to comply with international law; they change the public discourse on state actions into a debate that is shaped by international norms. As argued in Chapter 4 of the book, international courts shape the complicated network of global actors in numerous ways that strengthen the impact of international law.

This is why current scholarship isn't preoccupied only with state compliance with international courts. Scholars realized that international courts do much more than command states to change their behavior. The effectiveness of courts is determined by their capacity to fulfill multiple goals, including supporting legal regimes and enhancing their legitimacy.[30] The authority of international courts crucially depends on their interactions with their audiences and is not simply determined by international courts themselves.[31]

The complexity of the formal and informal networks that make international law isn't a bad thing. It is essential for ensuring global checks and balances that can prevent an excessive concentration of power. But this complexity does have disadvantages. It implies that central planning is impossible and no one is accountable for the policy decisions that shape the global arena.

The growing field of Global Administrative Law attempted to set principles for international governance that can overcome this accountability deficit. These principles include: transparency, participation, reasoned decisions, legality, and review mechanisms.[32] International courts may not get a perfect score on all these parameters –

[28] *See generally* Mark Granovetter, *Economic Action and Social Structure: The Problem of Embeddedness*, 91 Amer. J. Socio. 481 (1985).

[29] *See* Pauwelyn et al., Note 24, Chapter 4 at 3.

[30] *See generally* Shany, Note 12, Chapter 2.

[31] *See generally* Karen J. Alter, Laurence R. Helfer, & Mikael Rask Madsen, *How Context Shapes the Authority of International Courts*, 79 L. & Contemp. Prob. 1 (2016).

[32] *See* Benedict Kingsbury, Nico Krisch, & Richard B. Stewart, *The Emergence of Global Administrative Law*, 68 Law & Contemp. Prob. 15, 17 (2005).

Chapter 5 showed how international courts struggle to ensure participation and some courts lack transparency and proper review mechanisms – but they certainly comply with them better than most alternatives. Where else can you find a body so dedicated to issuing reasoned judgments based on international law?[33] By forcing states to openly defend their policies in legal terms, international courts expose policy-making to public scrutiny. This is the best tool to ensure transparency and accountability and to prevent abuses of power.

C Overcoming Weaknesses and the Rules of the Game

All that isn't to deny that international courts have some weaknesses. For example, scholars have pointed out that international judges are often biased in favor of their home states.[34] This poses a threat to the legitimacy of international courts. But that threat was taken into account when these courts were constructed. It is part of the reason why there are multiple judges in most panels making important decisions, and these judges come from different countries. As far as we know from empirical research, the number of cases decided a certain way because of judges' national bias is negligible.[35]

This book strives to show that regardless of the individual abilities of international judges – whether they are talented, experienced, and dedicated or not – institutional structures and established doctrines often allow international courts to make good judgments.

True, sometimes these institutional structures fail and bad judgments are issued. But life, paraphrasing a famous saying by Isaac Asimov, is different from most team sports. In life, the game goes on even after the judge announces the result.

[33] *See* Shai Dothan & Joanna Jemielniak, *A Paradigm Shift? Arbitration and Court-Like Mechanisms in Investors' Disputes forthcoming* Eur. YB. Int'l Economic L. (2020). (suggesting the advantages in terms of normative legitimacy of court-like mechanisms over arbitration to settle investment disputes).

[34] *See* Eric A. Posner & Miguel F. P. de Figueiredo, *Is the International Court of Justice Biased?* 34 J. Legal Stud. 599, 608 (2005).

[35] *See, e.g.*, Erik Voeten, *The Impartiality of International Judges: Evidence from the European Court of Human Rights*, 102 am. Pol. Sci. Rev. 417, 426 (2008).

BIBLIOGRAPHY

Books

Bruce Ackerman & James Fishkin, Deliberation Day (2004).

Aharon Barak, Judicial Discretion (1987) (Hebrew).

Purposive Interpretation in Law (2003) (Hebrew).

Ed Bates, The Evolution of the European Convention on Human Rights – From Its Inception to the Creation of a Permanent Court of Human Rights (2010).

Eyal Benvenisti, The Law of Global Governance (2014).

Alexander M. Bickel, The Least Dangerous Branch – The Supreme Court at the Bar of Politics (2d ed., 1986).

Eirik Bjorge, The Evolutionary Interpretation of Treaties (2014).

Armin von Bogdandy & Ingo Venzke, In Whose Name? A Public Law Theory of International Adjudication (2014).

Bill Bowring, The Degradation of the International Legal Order? The Rehabilitation of Law and the Possibility of Politics (2008).

Ronald S. Burt, Brokerage and Closure: An Introduction to Social Capital (2005).

Comparative International Law (Anthea Roberts et al., eds., 2018).

Lisa J. Conant, Justice Contained: Law and Politics in the European Union (2002).

Kanstantsin Dzehtsiarou, European Consensus and the Legitimacy of the European Court of Human Rights (2015)

P. Van Dijk & G. J. H. Van Hoof, Theory and Practice of the European Convention on Human Rights (3d ed., 1998).

Yoram Dinstein, International Treaties (1974) (Hebrew).

Shai Dothan, Reputation and Judicial Tactics: A Theory of National and International Courts (2015).

John Hart Ely, Democracy and Distrust – A Theory of Judicial Review (1980).

Federico Fabbrini, Fundamental Rights in Europe: Challenges and Transformations in a Comparative Perspective (2014).

Jack L. Goldsmith & Eric A. Posner, The Limits of International Law (2005).

Donna Gomien, David Harris, & Leo Zwaak, Law and Practice of the European Convention on Human Rights and the European Social Charter (1996).

Andrew T. Guzman, How International Law Works – A Rational Choice Theory (2008).

D. J. Harris, M. O'boyle, & C. Warbrick, Law of the European Convention on Human Rights (1995).

Courtney Hillebrecht, Domestic Politics and International Human Rights Tribunals: The Problem of Compliance (2014)

Albert O. Hirschman, Exit, Voice, and Loyalty – Responses to Decline in Firms, Organizations, and States (1970).

Loveday Hodson, NGOs and the Struggle for Human Rights in Europe (2011).

John Maynard Keynes, The General Theory of Employment, Interest and Money (2008).

Jann K. Kleffner, Complementarity in the Rome Statute and National Criminal Jurisdictions (2008).

Martti Koskenniemi, From Apology to Utopia: The Structure of International Legal Argument (2005).

Thomas Kuhn, The Structure of Scientific Revolutions (1962).

Hersch Lauterpacht, The Development of International Law by the International Court (1958).

Andrew Legg, The Margin of Appreciation in International Human Rights Law: Deference and Proportionality (2012).

J. G. Merrills, The Development of International Law by the European Court of Human Rights (2d ed.,1993).

Mancur Olson, The Logic of Collective Action (1965).

The Rise and Decline of Nations: Economic Growth, Stagflation, and Social Rigidities (1982).

Alexander Orakhelashvili, The Interpretation of Acts and Rules in Public International Law (2008).

Clare Ovey & Robin C. A. White, Jacobs & White: The European Convention on Human Rights (4th ed., 2006).

Eric A. Posner, The Perils of Global Legalism (2009).

Susanne K. Schmidt, The European Court of Justice and the Policy Process: The Shadow of Case Law (2018).

Jeffrey A. Segal & Harold J. Spaeth, The Supreme Court and the Attitudinal Model Revisited (2002).

Ivan. A. Shearer Starke's International Law (11th ed., 1994).

KATHRYN SIKKINK, THE JUSTICE CASCADE: HOW HUMAN RIGHTS PROSECUTIONS ARE CHANGING WORLD POLITICS (2011).

ANNE-MARIE SLAUGHTER, A NEW WORLD ORDER (2004).

THE CHESSBOARD AND THE WEB: STRATEGIES OF CONNECTION IN A NETWORKED WORLD (2017).

CASS. R. SUNSTEIN & REID HASTIE, WISER: GETTING BEYOND GROUPTHINK TO MAKE GROUPS SMARTER (2015).

ALEC STONE SWEET, GOVERNING WITH JUDGES: CONSTITUTIONAL POLITICS IN EUROPE (2000).

THE INTERNATIONAL COURT: CHALLENGES TO ACHIEVING JUSTICE AND ACCOUNTABILITY IN THE 21ST CENTURY (Mark S. Ellis & Richard J. Goldstone, eds., 2008).

ADRIAN VERMEULE, LAW AND THE LIMITS OF REASON (2009).

Articles

Oddný Mjöll Arnardóttir, *The Brighton Aftermath and the Changing Role of the European Court of Human Rights*, 9 J. INT'L DISPUTE SETTLEMENT 223 (2018).

Bruce A. Ackerman, *Beyond Carolene Products*, 98 HARV. L. REV. 713 (1985).

James F. Alexander, *The International Criminal Court and the Prevention of Atrocities: Predicting the Court's Impact*, 54 VILL. L. REV. 1 (2009).

Karen J. Alter, Laurence R. Helfer, & Mikael Rask Madsen, *How Context Shapes the Authority of International Courts*, 79 L. & CONTEMP. PROB. 1 (2016).

Karen J. Alter & Jeannette Vargas, *Explaining Variation in the Use of European Litigation Strategies: European Community Law and British Gender Equality Policy*, 33 COMP. POL. STUD. 452 (2000).

The Differences that Make a Difference: Recent Developments on the Discrimination Grounds and the Margin of Appreciation under Article 14 of the European Convention on Human Rights, 14 HUM. RTS. L. REV. 647 (2014).

Or Bassok, *Missing in Action: The Human Eye in* CONSTITUTIONS ACROSS BORDERS IN THE STRUGGLE AGAINST TERRORISM 283 (Federico Fabbrini & Vicki Jackson, eds., 2016).

Or Bassok & Yoav Dotan, *Solving the Countermajoritarian Difficulty?* 11 INT'L J. CONN. LAW 13 (2013).

Eyal Benvenisti, *Exit and Voice in the Age of Globalization*, 98 MICH. L. REV. 167 (1999).

Judicial Misgivings Regarding the Application of International Law: An Analysis of Attitudes of National Courts, 4 EUR. J. INT'L. L. 159 (1993).

Judicial Review and Democratic Failures: Minimizing Asymmetric Information through Adjudication, 32 TEL. AVIV. UNI. L. REV. 277 (Hebrew) (2010).

Margin of Appreciation, Consensus and Universal Standards, 31 NYU J. INT'L L. POL. 843, 849 (1999).

Reclaiming Democracy: The Strategic Uses of Foreign and International Law by National Courts, 102 AMER. J. INT'L L. 241 (2008).

Sovereigns as Trustees of Humanity: On the Accountability of States to Foreign Stakeholders, 107 AMER. J. INT'L L. 295 (2013).

Eyal Benvenisti & George W. Downs, *National Courts, Domestic Democracy, and the Evolution of International Law*, 20 EUR. J. INT'L L. 59 (2009).

The Premises, Assumptions and Implications of Van Gend en Loos: *Viewed from the Perspectives of Democracy and Legitimacy of International Institutions*, 25 EUR. J. INT'L L. 85 (2014).

Rudolf Bernhardt, *Evolutive Treaty Interpretation, Especially of the European Convention on Human Rights*, 42 GERMAN Y. B. INT'L L. 11 (1999).

Lisa Bernstein, *Opting Out of The Legal System: Extralegal Contractual Relations in the Diamond Industry*, 21 J. LEGAL STUD. 115 (1992).

Jeffrey A. Brauch, *The Margin of Appreciation and the Jurisprudence of the European Court of Human Rights: Threat to the Rule of Law*, 11 COLUM. J. EUR. L. 113 (2005).

Herbert W. Briggs, *United States Ratification of the Vienna Treaty Convention*, 73 AMER. J. I. L. 470 (1979).

Gonzalo Candia, *Comparing Diverse Approaches to the Margin of Appreciation: The Case of the European and the Inter-American Court of Human Rights*, available at: http://papers.ssrn.com/sol3/papers.cfm?abstract_id=2406705.

Paolo G. Carozza, *Uses and Misuses of Comparative Law in International Human Rights: Some Reflections on the Jurisprudence of the European Court of Human Rights*, 73 NOTRE DAME L. REV. 1217 (1998).

Stéphanie Cartier & Cristina Hoss, *The Role of Registries and Legal Secretariats in International Judicial Institutions*, *in* THE OXFORD HANDBOOK OF INTERNATIONAL ADJUDICATION 712 (Cesare P.R. Romano et al., eds., 2013).

James L. Cavallaro & Stephanie Erin Brewer, *Reevaluating Regional Human Rights Litigation in the Twenty-First Century: The Case of the Inter-American Court*, 102 AM. J. INT'L. L. 768 (2008).

Reevaluating Regional Human Rights Litigation in the Twenty-First Century: The Case of the Inter-American Court, 102 AM. J. INT'L. L. 768 (2008).

Abram Chayes, *The Role of the Judge in Public Law Litigation*, 89 HARV. L. REV. 1281 (1976).

Jacob Katz Cogan, *Competition and Control in International Adjudication*, 48 VA. J. INT'L L. 411 (2008).

Amichai Cohen, *Legal Operational Advice in the Israeli Defense Forces: The International Law Department and the Changing Nature of International Humanitarian Law*, 26 CONN. J. INT'L L. 367 (2011).

Hanoch Dagan, *The Realist Conception of Law*, 57 Uni. Toronto. L.J. 607 (2007).

David Davenport, *International Criminal Court: 12 Years, $1 Billion, 2 Convictions*, Forbes Mar. 12, 2014.

Sara Dezalay & Yves Dezalay, *Professionals of International Justice: From the Shadow of State Diplomacy to the Pull of the Market for Commercial Arbitration*, *in* International Law as a Profession 311 (eds. Jean D'Aspremont et al, 2017).

Shai Dothan, *The Advantage of International Courts*, 31 Bar Ilan University Law Review 675 (2018) (Hebrew).

Comparative Views on the Right to Vote in International Law: The Case of Prisoners' Disenfranchisement, *in* Comparative International Law 379 (Anthea Roberts et al., eds., Oxford University Press, 2018).

In Defence of Expansive Interpretation in the European Court of Human Rights, 3 Cambridge J. Int'l & Comp. L. 508 (2014).

Deterring War Crimes, 40 N. C. J. Int'l L. & Com. Reg. 739 (2015).

How International Courts Enhance Their Legitimacy, 14 Theo. Inq. L. 455 (2013).

International Courts Improve Public Deliberation, 39 Mich. J. Int'l L. 217 (2018).

Judicial Tactics in the European Court of Human Rights, 12 Chi. J. Int'l. L. 115 (2011).

Luring NGOs to International Courts: A Comment on CLR v. Romania, 75 Heidelberg J. Int'l L. 635 (2015).

The Motivations of Individual Judges and How They Act as a Group, 19 German L.J. 2165 (2018).

The Optimal Use of Comparative Law, 43 Denv. J. Int'l L. & Pol'y. 21 (2014).

Social Networks and the Enforcement of International Law, *in* Edward Elgar Research Handbook on the Sociology of International Law 333 (Moshe Hirsch & Andrew Lang, eds., 2018).

Three Interpretive Constraints on the European Court of Human Rights, *in* The Rule of Law at the National and International Levels: Contestations and Deference 227 (Machiko Kanetake & André Nollkaemper, eds., Hart Publishing, 2016).

The Three Traditional Approaches to Treaty Interpretation: A Current Application to the European Court of Human Rights, 42 Fordham Int'l L.J. 765 (2019).

A Virtual Wall of Shame: The New Way of Imposing Reputational Sanctions on Defiant States, 27 Duke J. Comp. & Int'l. L. 141 (2017).

Shai Dothan & Joanna Jemielniak, *A Paradigm Shift? Arbitration and Court-Like Mechanisms in Investors' Disputes forthcoming* Eur. YB. Int'l Economic L. (2020).

Jeffrey L. Dunoff & Joel P. Trachtman, *The Law and Economics of Humanitarian Law Violations in Internal Conflict*, 93 AMER. J. INT'L L. 394 (1999).

Susan Easton, *The Prisoner's Right to Vote and Civic Responsibility: Reaffirming the Social Contract?* 56 PROBATION J. 224 (2009).

Harry J. Enten, *Felon Voting Rights Have a Bigger Impact on Elections than Voter ID Laws*, THE GUARDIAN July 31, 2013.

Lee Epstein, Jack Knight, & Andrew D. Martin, *The Political (Science) Context of Judging*, 47 ST. LOUIS U. L.J. 783 (2003).

William N. Eskridge, Jr., *Reneging on History? Playing the Court/Congress/President Civil Rights Game*, 79 CAL. L. REV. 613 (1991).

Owen M. Fiss, *Foreword: The Forms of Justice*, 93 HARV. L. REV. 1 (1979).

The Social and Political Foundations of Adjudication, 6 LAW & HUM. BEHAV. 121 (1982).

Malgosia Fitzmaurice & Panos Merkouris, *Canons of Treaty Interpretation: Selected Case Studies from the World Trade Organization and the North American Free Trade Agreement*, *in* TREATY INTERPRETATION AND THE VIENNA CONVENTION ON THE LAW OF TREATIES: 30 YEARS ON 153 (Malgosia Fitzmaurice et al., eds., 2010).

Milton Friedman, *The Methodology of Positive Economics*, ESSAYS IN POSITIVE ECONOMICS 3 (1953).

Lon L. Fuller, *The Forms and Limits of Adjudication*, 92 HARV. L. REV. 353 (1978).

Howard Gillman, *What's Law Got to Do with It? Judicial Behavioralists Test the "Legal Model" of Judicial Decision Making*, 26 L. & SOC. INQUIRY 465 (2001).

Tom Ginsburg, *Bounded Discretion in International Judicial Lawmaking*, 45 VA. J. INT'L L. 631 (2005).

Eastphalia as the Perfection of Westphalia, 17 IND. J. GLOBAL LEGAL STUD. 27 (2010).

Tom Ginsburg & Richard H. McAdams, *Adjudication in Anarchy: an Expressive Theory of International Dispute Resolution*, 45 WM & MARY L. REV. 1229 (2004).

Mark Granovetter, *Economic Action and Social Structure: The Problem of Embeddedness*, 91 AMER. J. SOCIO. 481 (1985).

Threshold Models of Collective Behavior, 83 AMER. J. SOC. 1420 (1978).

Peter M. Haas, *Introduction: Epistemic Communities and International Policy Coordination*, 46 INT'L ORG. 1 (1992).

Terence C. Halliday, Lucien Karpik, & Malcolm Feeley, *Introduction: the Legal Complex in Struggles for Political Liberalism*, *in* FIGHTING FOR POLITICAL FREEDOM: COMPARATIVE STUDIES OF THE LEGAL COMPLEX AND POLITICAL CHANGE 1 (Terence C. Halliday, Lucien Karpik, & Malcolm Feeley, eds., 2007).

Oona A. Hathaway, *Between Power and Principle: An Integrated Theory of International Law*, 72 U. Chi. L. Rev. 469 (2005).

Laurence R. Helfer & Anne-Marie Slaughter, *Toward a Theory of Effective Supranational Adjudication*, 107 Yale L.J. 273 (1997).

Why States Create International Tribunals: A Response to Professors Posner and Yoo, 93 Cal. L. Rev. 899 (2005).

Laurence R. Helfer & Erik Voeten, *International Courts as Agents of Legal Change: Evidence from LGBT Rights in Europe*, 68 Int'l Org. 77 (2014).

Kevin Jon Heller, *A Sentence-Based Theory of Complementarity*, 53 Harv. Int'l L.J. 85 (2012).

Simon Hentrei, *Generalising the Principle of Complementarity: Framing International Judicial Authority*, 4 Trans. Leg. Theo. 419 (2013).

Lord Hoffmann, *The Universality of Human Rights*, Judicial Studies Board Annual Lecture, Mar. 19, 2009, available at https://conservativehome.blogs.com/files/hoffmann_2009_jsb_annual_lecture_universality_of_human_rights.pdf.

Andreas Hofmann, *Is the Commission Levelling the Playing Field? Rights Enforcement in the European Union*, 40 J. Eur. Integration 737 (2018).

Jakob von Holderstein Holtermann, *A "Slice of Cheese" – A Deterrence-Based Argument for the International Criminal Court*, 11 Hum. Rts. Rev. 289 (2010).

Andrew Hough, *Prisoner Vote: What MPs Said in Heated Debate*, The Telegraph, Feb. 11, 2011.

Alexandra Huneeus, *Courts Resisting Courts: Lessons from the Inter-American Court's Struggle to Enforce Human Rights*, 44 Cornell Int'l. L.J. 493 (2011).

International Criminal Law by Other Means: The Quasi-Criminal Jurisdiction of International Courts, 107 Am. J. Int'l L. 1 (2013).

Joshua L. Jackson, *Broniowski v. Poland: A Recipe for Increased Legitimacy of the European Court of Human Rights as a Supranational Constitutional Court*, 39 Conn. L. Rev. 759 (2006).

Francis G. Jacobs, *Varieties of Approach to Treaty Interpretation: With Special Reference to the Draft Convention on the Law of Treaties before the Vienna Diplomatic Conference*, 18 Int'l. & Comp. L.Q. 318 (1969).

Benedict Kingsbury, Nico Krisch, & Richard B. Stewart, *The Emergence of Global Administrative Law*, 68 Law & Contemp. Prob. 15 (2005).

Martti Koskenniemi, *The Politics of International Law*, 1 Eur. J. Int'l L. 4 (1990).

Lewis A. Kornhauser & Lawrence G. Sager, *Unpacking the Court*, 96 Yale L.J. 82 (1986).

David Kosař, *Selecting Strasburg Judges, in* Selecting Europe's Judges: A Critical Review of the Appointment Procedures to the European Courts (Michal Bobek, ed., 2015).

Harold Hongju Koh, *How Is International Human Rights Law Enforced?* 74 Ind. L.J. 1397 (1999).

Julian Ku & Jide Nzelibe, *Do International Criminal Tribunals Deter or Exacerbate Humanitarian Atrocities*, 84 Wash. U. L. Rev. 777 (2006).

Edward O. Laumann & Yoosik Youm, *Racial/Ethnic Group Differences in the Prevalence of Sexually Transmitted Diseases in the United States: A Network Explanation*, 26 Sexually Transmitted Diseases 250 (1999).

Hersch Lauterpacht, *Restrictive Interpretation and the Principle of Effectiveness in the Interpretation of Treaties*, 26 Brit. Y.B. Int'l. L. 48 (1949).

David S. Law, *A Theory of Judicial Power and Judicial Review*, 97 Geo. L.J. 723 (2009).

Scott Leckie, *The Inter-State Complaint Procedure in International Human Rights Law: Hopeful Prospects or Wishful Thinking?* 10 Hum. Rts Q. 249 (1988).

Ulf Linderfalk, *Is the Hierarchical Structure of Articles 31 and 32 of the Vienna Convention Real or Not? Interpreting the Rules of Interpretation*, 54 Netherlands Int'l L. Rev. 133 (2007).

Susanne Lohmann, *An Information Rationale for the Power of Special Interests*, 92 Amer. Pol. Sci. Rev. 809 (1998).

Mikael Rask Madsen, *Rebalancing European Human Rights: Has the Brighton Declaration Engendered a New Deal on Human Rights in Europe*, 9 J. Int'l Dispute Settlement 199 (2018).

Paul Mahoney, *Judicial Activism and Judicial Self-Restraint in the European Court of Human Rights: Two Sides of the Same Coin*, 11 Hum. R. L.J. 57 (1990).

F. Matscher, *Methods of Interpretation of the Convention*, *in* The European System for The Protection of Human Rights 63 (R. St. J. Macdonald, F. Matscher, and H. Petzold, eds., 1993).

Menachem Mautner, *Luck in Courts*, 9 Theo. Inq. L. 217 (2007).

Mathew D. McCubbins & Thomas Scwartz, *Congressional Oversight Overlooked: Police Patrols versus Fire Alarms*, 28 Amer. J. Pol. Sci. 165 (1984).

Dominic McGoldrick, *Criminal Trials before International Tribunals: Legality and Legitimacy in* The Permanent International Criminal Court: Legal and Policy Issues (Studies in International Law) (Eric Donnelly, Dominic McGoldrick, and Peter J. Rowe, eds.) 9 (2004).

Lucja Miara & Victoria Prais, *The Role of Civil Society in the Execution of Judgments of the European Court of Human Rights*, 5 Eur. Hum. Rt. L. Rev. 528 (2012).

Frank I. Michelman, *The Constitution, Social Rights, and Liberal Political Justification*, 1 I-CON 13 (2003).

Andrew Moravcsik, *The Origins of Human Rights Regimes: Democratic Delegation in Postwar Europe*, 54 Int'l Org. 217 (2000).

Rory O'Connell, *Cinderella Comes to the Ball: Art 14 and the Right to Non-discrimination in the ECHR*, 29 LEG. STUD. 211 (2009).

Alexander Orakhelashvili, *Restrictive Interpretation of Human Rights Treaties in the Recent Jurisprudence of the European Court of Human Rights*, 14 EUR. J. INT'L L. 529 (2003).

François Ost, *The Original Canons of Interpretation of the European Court of Human Rights*, *in* THE EUROPEAN CONVENTION FOR THE PROTECTION OF HUMAN RIGHTS: INTERNATIONAL PROTECTION VERSUS NATIONAL RESTRICTIONS 283 (Mireille Delmas-Marty, ed., 1992).

Joost Pauwelyn, Ramses A. Wessel, & Jan Wouters, *An Introduction to Informal International Lawmaking*, *in* INFORMAL INTERNATIONAL LAWMAKING 1 (Joost Pauwelyn, Ramses A. Wessel, & Jan Wouters, eds., 2012).

Anne Peters, *Humanity as the A and Ω of. Sovereignty*, 20 EUR. J. INT'L L. 513 (2009).

Mitchell Polinsky & Steven Shavell, *The Economic Theory of Public Enforcement of Law*, 38 J. ECON. LIT. 45 (2000).

Dragoljub Popovic, *Prevailing of Judicial Activism over Self-Restraint in the Jurisprudence of the European Court of Human Rights*, 42 CREIGHTON L. REV. 361 (2009).

Eric Posner & Cass Sunstein, *The Law of Other States*, 59 STAN. L. REV. 131 (2006).

Eric A. Posner & John C. Yoo, *Judicial Independence in International Tribunals*, 93 CAL. L. REV. 1 (2005).

Eric A. Posner & Miguel F. P. de Figueiredo, *Is the International Court of Justice Biased?* 34 J. LEGAL STUD. 599 (2005).

Dirk Pulkowski, *Structural Paradigms of International law*, *in* THE SHIFTING ALLOCATION OF AUTHORITY IN INTERNATIONAL LAW: CONSIDERING SOVEREIGNTY, SUPREMACY AND SUBSIDIARITY 51 (Tomer Broude & Yuval Shany, eds., 2008).

Robert D. Putnam, *Diplomacy and Domestic Politics: The Logic of Two-Level Games*, 42 INT'L ORG. 427 (1988).

Yaël Ronen & Yael Naggan, *Third Parties*, *in* THE OXFORD HANDBOOK OF INTERNATIONAL ADJUDICATION 806 (Cesare Romano, Karen Alter, & Yuval Shany, eds., 2013).

Alexandra Ruth and Mirja Trilsch, *Bankovic v. Belgium (Admissibility)*, 97 AM. J. INT'L L 168 (2003).

Frederick Schauer, *Do Cases Make Bad Law?* 73 UNI CHI. L. REV 883 (2006).

Gregory Shaffer & Tom Ginsburg, *The Empirical Turn in International Legal Scholarship*, 106 AM. J. INT'L L. 1 (2012).

Yuval Shany, *Assessing the Effectiveness of International Courts: A Goal-Based Approach*, 106 AMER. J. INT'L. L. 225 (2012).

Toward a General Margin of Appreciation Doctrine in International Law? 16 Eur. J. Int'l L. 907 (2006).

Dinah Shelton, *The Participation of Nongovernmental Organizations in International Judicial Proceedings*, 88 Am. J. Int'l. L. 611 (1994).

Beth A. Simmons & Allison Danner, *Credible Commitments and the International Criminal Court*, 64 Int'l Org. 225 (2010).

James Slack, *Social Ties Keep Rapists in Britain*, Mail On Line Sept. 21, 2011.

Robert Spano, *Universality or Diversity of Human Rights: Strasburg in the Age of Subsidiarity*, 14 Hum. Rts. L. Rev. 487 (2014).

Andreas von Staden, *The Democratic Legitimacy of Judicial Review beyond the State: Normative Subsidiarity and Judicial Standards of Review*, 10 Int'l J. Con. L. 1023 (2012).

Maxwell L. Stearns, *The Condorcet Jury Theorem and Judicial Decisionmaking: A Reply to Saul Levmore*, 3 Theo. Inq. L. 125 (2002).

Øyvind Stiansen, *Competition and Compliance: Electoral Uncertainty and Implementation of Judgments from the International Human Rights Judiciary* (draft available at https://papers.ssrn.com/sol3/papers.cfm?abstract_id=3116708).

Lord Sumption, The 27th Sultan Azlan Shah Lecture, Kuala Lumpur: The Limits of Law (Nov. 20, 2013), www.supremecourt.uk/docs/speech-131120.pdf.

Cass R. Sunstein, *Deliberative Trouble? Why Groups Go to Extremes*, 110 Yale L.J. 71 (2000).

James B. Thayer, *The Origin and Scope of the American Doctrine of Constitutional Law*, 7 Harv. L. Rev. 129 (1893).

Peter Van den Bossche, *NGO Involvement in the WTO: A Comparative Perspective*, 11 J. Int'l. Econ. L. 717, 721 (2008).

Antoine Vauchez, *Communities of International Litigators*, *in* The Oxford Handbook of International Adjudication 655 (Cesare P. R. Romano et al., eds., 2013).

Erik Voeten, *Public Opinion and the Legitimacy of International Courts*, 14 Theo. Inq. L. 411 (2013).

The Impartiality of International Judges: Evidence from the European Court of Human Rights, 102 am. Pol. Sci. Rev. 417 (2008).

The Politics of International Judicial Appointments: Evidence from the European Court of Human Rights, 61 Int'l. Org. 669 (2007).

Jeremy Waldron, *Are Sovereigns Entitled to the Benefit of the International Rule of Law*, 22 Eur. J. Int'l L. 315 (2011).

The Core of the Case against Judicial Review, 115 Yale L.J. 1346 (2006).

Tim Worstall, *Misunderstanding Brexit–Scrapping the Human Rights Act for a British Bill of Rights*, Forbes Aug. 23, 2016.

Treaties

American Convention on Human Rights
Convention for the Protection of Human Rights and Fundamental Freedoms
Rome Statute of the International Criminal Court
Statute of the Council of Europe
Statute of the International Court of Justice
Statute of the International Criminal Tribunal for Rwanda
The Treaty on the Functioning of the European Union
Updated Statute of the International Criminal Tribunal for the Former Yugoslavia
Vienna Convention on Consular Relations
Vienna Convention on the Law of Treaties

Judgments

European Court of Human Rights

Case of *A. A.* v. *The United Kingdom*, judgment of September 20, 2011.

Case of *A, B, and C* v. *Ireland*, judgment of December 16, 2010.

Case of *Abdulaziz, Cabales and Balkandali* v. *The United Kingdom*, judgment of May 28, 1985 EUR. Ct. H.R. (ser. A) 94.

Airey v. *Ireland*, judgment of October 9, 1979, EUR. Ct. H.R. (ser. A)32.

Al-Jedda v. *The United Kingdom*, Judgment of July 7, 2011, Reports of Judgments and Decisions EUR. Ct. H.R. 2011.

Al-Skeini and Others v. *The United Kingdom*, Judgment of July 7, 2011, Reports of Judgments and Decisions EUR. Ct. H.R. 2011.

Artico v. *Italy*, judgment of May 13, 1980 EUR. Ct. H.R. (ser. A)37.

Bankovic and others v. *Belgium and Others*, Decision of December 12, 2001, EUR. Ct. H.R. 2001-XII 333

Broniowski v. *Poland*, judgment of June 22, 2004, 2004-V EUR. Ct. H.R. 1.

Cossey case, judgment of September 27, 1990 EUR. Ct. H.R. (ser. A) 184.

CLR v. *Romania*, judgment of July 17, 2014, Reports of Judgments and Decisions EUR. Ct. H.R. 2014.

Cyprus v. *Turkey*, Judgment of May 10, 2001, *Reports of Judgments and Decisions*, 2001-IV.

Case of *D. H. and Others* v. *The Czech Republic*, judgment of February 7, 2006.

Case of *D. H. and Others* v. *The Czech Republic*, judgment of November 11, 2011, Reports of Judgments and Decisions 2007-IV.

Case of *Dickson* v. *The United Kingdom*, judgment of December 4, 2007.

Dudgeon v. *The United Kingdom*, judgment of October 22, 1981 EUR. Ct. H.R. (ser. A) 45.

Case of *Evans* v. *The United Kingdom*, judgment of April 10, 2007.

Fairfield and Others v. *The United Kingdom*, Decision of March 8, 2005.

Golder v. *The United Kingdom*, App. No. 4451/70, Eur. Comm'n H.R., (ser. B no. 16) 1 June 1973.

Case of *Golder* v. *The United Kingdom* judgment of February 21, 1975 EUR. Ct. H.R. (ser. A)18.

Christine Goodwin v. *The United Kingdom*, judgment of July 11, 2002, 2002-VI EUR. Ct. H.R. 1.

Greens and MT v. *United Kingdom*, judgment of November 23, 2010, Reports of Judgments and Decisions 2010.

Case of *Haas* v. *The Netherlands*, judgment of January 13, 2004, Reports of Judgments and Decisions 2004-I.

Hirst v. *The United Kingdom* (No. 2), judgment of October 6, 2005, 2005-IX EUR. Ct. H.R. 187.

Case of *Ireland* v. *The United Kingdom*, judgment of January 18, 1978 EUR. Ct. H.R. (ser. A) 25.

Case of Klass and others Judgment of September 6, 1978 EUR. Ct. H.R. (ser. A)28.

Case of *Leyla Sahin* v. *Turkey*, judgment of November 10, 2005.

Case of *Loizidou* v. *Turkey* (Preliminary Objections) Judgment of March 23, 1995, EUR. Ct. H.R. (ser.A) 310.

Case of *Loizidou* v. *Turkey*, judgment of December 18, 1996 (merits) *Reports of Judgments and Decisions* 1996-VI.

Marckx v. *Belgium*, Judgment of June 13, 1979 EUR. Ct. H.R. (ser. A)31.

Minelli v. *Switzerland*, judgment of March 25, 1983, EUR. Ct. H.R. (ser. A)62.

Case of *Othman (Abu Qatada)* v. *The United Kingdom*, judgment of January 17, 2012, Reports of Judgments and Decisions 2012.

Case "relating to certain aspects of the laws on the use of languages in education in Belgium" judgment of July 23, 1968 EUR. Ct. H.R. (ser. A) 6.

Rees v. *The United Kingdom*, judgment of October 17, 1986 EUR. Ct. H.R. (ser. A) 106.

S.A.S v. *France*, judgment of July 1, 2014

Sheffield and Horsham v. *The United Kingdom*, judgment of July 30, 1998, 1998-V EUR. Ct. H.R. 2011.

Soering case, judgment of 7 July 1989, EUR. Ct. H.R (ser. A)161.

Case of *Stec and Others* v. *The United Kingdom*, judgment of April 12, 2006, Reports of Judgments and Decisions 2006-VI.

Grand Chamber Decision as to the Admissibility of Applications nos. 65731/01 and 65900/01 by *Stec and Others* v. *The United Kingdom*.

Tyrer case, judgment of April 25, 1978 EUR. Ct. H.R. (ser. A) 26.

Van der Mussele v. *Belgium*, judgment of November 23, 1983 EUR. Ct. H.R. (ser. A)70.

Von Hannover v. *Germany*, 2004-III Eur. Ct. H.R. 1.

Case of *Wemhoff* v. *Germany* judgment of June 27, 1968 EUR. Ct. H.R. (ser. A) 7.

X and Y v. *The Netherlands*, Judgment of March 26, 1985 EUR. Ct. H.R. (ser. A)91.

International Criminal Court

Judgment on the appeal of the Republic of Kenya against the decision of Pre-trial Chamber II of May 30, 2011 entitled "Decision on the Application by the Government of Kenya Challenging the Admissibility of the Case Pursuant to Article 19(2)(b) of the Statute," Situation in the Republic of Kenya (Muthaura, Kenyatta, and Ali) (ICC-01/09–02/11 OA), Appeals Chamber, Aug. 30, 2011.

Prosecutor v. *Saif Al-Islam Gaddafi & Abdullah Al-Senussi*, Case No. ICC-01/11-01/11, Pre-trial Chamber I Decision Requesting Further Submissions on Issues Related to the Admissibility of the Case against Saif Al-Islam Gaddafi, 5–19 (Dec. 7, 2012).

International Criminal Tribunal for the Former Yugoslavia

Prosecutor v. *Erdemovic*, IT-96-22-T ICTY Trial Chamber I (1996) at par. 19.

Court of Justice of the European Union

Rewe Zentrale AG v. Bundesmonopolverwaltung für Branntwein C-120/78, (1979) European court Reports (E.C.R.), 649.

Case C-402/05P and C-415/05P. Kadi and Al Barakaat International Foundation v. Council and Commission [2008] ECR I-6351

Case C-584/10P, C-593/10P, and C 595/10P Commission v. Kadi, judgment of July 18, 2013.

International Court of Justice

Case Concerning Avena and Other Mexican Nationals (Mex. v. U.S.), [2004] ICJ Rep. 12.

World Trade Organization Appellate Body

WTO Appellate Body Report, United States – Import Prohibition of Certain Shrimp and Shrimp Products WT/DS58/AB/R (12 Oct. 1998)

United States Supreme Court

Bowers v. *Hardwick*, 478 U.S. 186 (1986).

Lawrence v. *Texas*, 539 U.S. 558 (2003).

Medellin v. *Texas*, 552 U.S. 491 (2008).

United States v. *Carolene Products Co.*, 304 U.S. 144 (1938).

High Court of Australia

The State of New South Wales v. *Amery and Others*, [2006] HCA 14 par. 168–171.

Israeli Supreme Court

HCJ 5100/94 *Public Committee against Torture* v. *Israel* [1999] IsrSC 53(4) 817.

INDEX